Your House
Their House

Your House
Their House

THE BEST AND WORST OF RESIDENTIAL CHILD CARE

Thomas Daubert

authorHOUSE®

AuthorHouse™
1663 Liberty Drive
Bloomington, IN 47403
www.authorhouse.com
Phone: 1-800-839-8640

First published by AuthorHouse   07/12/2011

ISBN: 978-1-4634-3487-8 (sc)
ISBN: 978-1-4634-3486-1 (ebk)

Library of Congress Control Number: 201191212920

Printed in the United States of America

INTRODUCTION

Of the near twenty years I have been in the field of education, eighteen of them were spent working in residential facilities. The first school I spent nearly sixteen years working there, but the second one I was only there for a year and a half. Was there a difference between the two schools? Absolutely yes! I also spent quite a bit of time applying, examining, and interviewing for a variety of other residential schools while at the two schools. The experience I gained during these eighteen years was enlightening and valuable, to say the least.

Residential facilities are larger in number than one might realize and many people may not understand what would motivate someone like me to work at one of these schools. There are definitely advantages to working at programs like these, which is why I spent the majority of my career working at one. Sadly, there are also some serious disadvantages and pitfalls in these types of organizations. I hope to enlighten those who may be looking into a career as a houseparent or teacher at a boarding school or residential facility just what these advantages or disadvantages are. Looking back, I wish that I would have known this information before I pursued certain positions, not that I regret the experience I gained.

To avoid mentioning specific names of the organizations where I worked, I will use fictitious names. For the school where I spent the majority of my time, I will call it Bright Meadows Academy and for the other organization where I only worked for a year and a half I will call it Dark Hills Academy. There have been publications in the not-to-distant past that have slandered organizations like these, but this work is not for this purpose whatsoever. However, there are some grim realities that need to be pointed out as well as some positive things to consider. Whether you are married or single, the advantages and disadvantages I believe are similar in amount.

PART 1:
GETTING STARTED

THE GREAT PROVIDERS

After student teaching, I got a job working at a small, Christian school in Pennsylvania. The first thing I noticed about this school, and about most Christian schools, is the small student enrollment. The school I taught at only had two people in its graduating class. The low student count provided a lower student to staff ratio, which was advantageous to more effective learning. Unfortunately, with lower student enrollment, these schools are unable to hire more teachers, which consequently require the present teaching staff to take on more responsibilities. I only had an average of six students per class, but I was teaching six different classes, all of which required the writing of lesson plans and the creating of tests and quizzes.

Organizations like these also cannot provide competitive salaries or benefits for teachers and their families. I eked out a meager living with my annual salary and thankfully I did not have the responsibility of providing for a family. In 2007 I surveyed hundreds of Christian school teachers and just about all of them gave glowing reviews about their teaching jobs. The biggest complaint revolved around low salaries and substandard health and retirement benefits. A friend of mine at a Christian preparatory school was telling me recently that he had to get a second job to better provide for his family.

The initial appeal of working as a house parent at a boarding school, Christian or otherwise, was the fact that the majority of them provided room and board, which is the largest single living expense. In addition, just about all of them provide meals for those that are on duty. A year and a half ago, when my wife and I were looking into various house parenting positions on-line, many of those listed also provided health and retirement benefits as well. In some cases, premiums were not even deducted from paychecks because the organizations covered this. In this day and age, with so much need prevalent, boarding schools need some kind of drawing power to entice quality staff into their organization.

Keep in mind that the housing provision is going to differ greatly from organization to organization. For example, one boarding school my wife and I looked into had beautiful, spacious living quarters, and another one we interviewed at had appliances and free internet in all of the relief rooms. There was another institution we saw that had only two bedrooms and no separate apartment for the housestaff to stay on their days off. Not only that, but there was no private bathroom for the house parents to use; they had to go out into the student residence to use the bathroom. Still, other organizations required the house parents to provide their own housing, which would have added significant financial burdens.

When I worked at Bright Meadows Academy, they did not have enough money to provide health care. Instead, they had different funds and financial aid that helped staff provide their own healthcare. The problem with this system was that it did not provide consistent coverage and the funds were eventually exhausted to a point that no more money was available. Other organizations had healthcare, but the amount deducted per pay period was so ridiculously high, that it was not worth it. As a single worker, healthcare was never really an issue, but once I was married with a child, it was a large concern that my family and I were provided in this way.

With room and board provided as well as other expenses, it made it easier for my wife and I to pay off long-term expenses like mortgages and college loans. As an employee at a small Christian school, I had to have parental help to pay for some of my other bills. When I worked at a boarding school overseas, I heard several staff members remark that they were able to pay off major expenses because there was nothing to really spend their money on, since most everything was provided for them. After working overseas and having very few living expenses, I was also able to buy a better car and pay for my own car insurance.

Some schools even offer incentives to further your education. When I worked at Bright Meadows, for every month I stayed beyond my two year contract, they gave one hundred dollars toward graduate school. They even helped me enroll in the graduate school and paid for it until graduation. Many schools are unable to offer this due to the financial hardships. As a rule, most organizations should offer some kind of training to help you become a better teacher or youth care worker.

THE MISSION

If you ask most people involved in child care why they pursued this line of work, they would tell you that it was to make a difference in the lives of children and teenagers. There is no question that now more than ever, young people face challenges in their lives. Factors such as poor academics, negative peer pressure, family crises, and mental and emotional trauma create the need for students to be taken out of a negative environment. Residential and boarding schools allow students to be taken out of a negative or distracting surrounding and put into a setting that is going to be more nurturing and more conducive to learning and self improvement. Overall, the demand for boys tends to be higher for boys than it does for girls. Girls are better able to adapt to negative environments, or at least do not act out as negatively. Boys tend to be more aggressive and more overt in their bad behavior. Although there are other reasons for the presence of boarding schools, the majority of them exist for behavioral reasons.

The thing to keep in mind is that if you are not passionate about your mission to help young people, working in a residential facility, particularly as a house parent, this line of work is not for you. Several years ago, I had a fellow teacher once tell me that he did not know why God called him into teaching. He shared that he did not particularly like young people and did not care about teaching on a daily basis. Nevertheless he was convinced that it was his calling. Speaking as a Christian, I firmly believe that God would never call you into something that you are not passionate about. Working as a residential youth care worker consumes your life and your being. Approaching it from a strictly employment perspective is totally wrong and will inevitably lead to frustration and burnout.

House parenting is the type of career that demands constant spiritual renewal, devout dedication to the mission, and hours of hard work. It is no wonder that that the average stay of a house parent is two years; for some organizations it is even less. House parenting usually attracts younger couples, newly married many times, who are zealous about working with young people. It may also attract older couples who have retired from their careers and who want a change in pace. Although some organizations may hire single people as youth care workers, most want married couples who have been married for a minimum of three years. It is not only important that the individual be dedicated to the mission, it is also important that the spouse be equally as dedicated. This way one can be an encouragement to the other when one is feeling discouraged or feeling like giving up.

A word of caution for those who are zealous about the mission of helping students: people who are excited about helping out for the first time tend to overdo it with the amount of work they volunteer for. I have known several youth care workers in my time who sign up for as many activities as possible in a fit of zeal. The problem with this that some people don't realize how much energy is required to do the regular house parenting job, let alone other activities. These workers are at a greater risk of job frustration and burnout, and many times their extra work is seldom recognized and appreciated.

CHOOSING THE RIGHT ONE

Once you feel the call of house parenting on your life, the next question is which one is going to be the best one for you. The most important thing to remember as a Christian is to allow God to work His will in your life. This career is not only a calling; it is a way of life. In most lines of work, one is able to leave the problems behind once they leave for home. It's amazing how much you think about work even when you are off duty because of the mental and emotional demands. Even though it will differ from place to place, be sure you are ready, willing, and able to handle these demands. Above all else, be in constant prayer about all decisions you make.

Probably the first place you are going to look for a house parenting position is on the internet, since it is the easiest and most productive method of looking. Without question, every residential facility's web site is going to show a plethora of pictures of shiny, smiling students and groups of students with their arms around each other. They will show beautiful pictures of the surroundings, whether they be of the geography or of the facility itself. As with any type of advertising, the main goal is to make the organization as visually stimulating as possible. Web sites that post job openings for house parents usually will lead you to the specific facility you click on. The point here is to get past the initial advertising and get right to the task at hand.

One of the most important things an effective youth care facility has is a solid philosophy and a clear mission statement. A philosophy is the reasoning behind what they do and a mission statement is what they actually do to reinforce their philosophy. There are so many organizations to choose from and many of them appear to be similar. The question is which ones have mission statements that jibe with your mission. It's also important to have a philosophy based on Biblical principals. Any school or Christian ministry should have a clearly defined purpose for its existence; otherwise it's nearly impossible to tell them apart and what they do may not be clearly understood. Mission statements should not be longer than one or two sentences, but be specific enough so that there is a distinction from other ministries and schools.

Another obvious thing you want to find out is which organization is hiring and which one is not. Just because a facility posts a position available does not necessarily mean that they are hiring at that moment. Many places will post a house parenting position available with no intent of immediate hire. One of the main reasons they do this is so they can keep a list of names available in case some of their employees decide to leave. Sometimes they simply do not remove the posting in a timely fashion. If the facility indeed sounds like one you would be interested in working in, call them up or e-mail them to find out if they are indeed actively looking for the positions posted. The ones who are not immediately hiring will probably say "Don't call us; we'll call you when the position opens." If that's the case, my suggestion is not to even bother. Most of the applications are way too lengthy to fill out only to have it put on a shelf indefinitely. If they are actively looking, find out how old the posting is and how soon they desire to have the position filled.

I am a firm believer that just as a truly evil person will never admit they are evil, a poorly managed facility will never admit to its shortcomings. It would definitely make life easier if you knew right off what the shortcomings of a prospective employer was before signing a contract. One way to bypass this is to read the mission statement of the organization. The mission statement should be clearly yet tersely written. Most youth care facilities will say something about changing kids' lives and making them outstanding students. It's a very noble goal, but the facility should also have a distinct philosophy as well as a clear mission statement. How do they intend to achieve their mission? It's one thing to have good intentions, but it should be clear from the web site or any mailed material how exactly they achieve their mission. What makes them different from all the many other boarding schools across the country?

How important is location? Most organizations I looked into seemed to be located either in the Southern or Western United States. My wife and I personally drew the line at a day's drive away. It really depends on how willing you are to move away from where you are now. There are even American based programs in foreign countries like Costa Rica or the Bahamas. If you are that committed to your mission, perhaps these organizations will be positive life changing experiences for you and your family. Just find out as much information as possible about the organization and how it runs. If you decide to stay in the United States, it would also be a good idea to find out about the cost of living of that area. Although most organizations provide many of the living expenses, you may still be responsible for expenses like gas or food. In our travels, we found towns outside of metropolitan areas to be very expensive. Yet another thing to consider is how far away it is from the nearest town or city. Many facilities like to be in somewhat isolated areas and although the scenery tends to be picturesque, being too far away from a major town can not only be an inconvenience, it could also be a hazard if emergency services are ever needed.

It's also important to find out the type of clientele the school accepts. I talked to a newly hired housefather who interviewed for a house parenting job somewhere in the Southwest. He did not accept the job because many of the students were older teenagers, some of whom had a tendency toward violence and a life of crime. He turned down the job because he did not feel the structure was tight enough to handle such a volatile population to a point where he felt like his and his wife's physical well-being could be jeopardized. My wife and I also interviewed for a residential facility for unwed teenage mothers. Even though our daughter was less than a year old, we didn't think anything about working with this type of girls. I was thankful we weren't hired because I couldn't see raising our daughter while simultaneously helping other girls raise theirs. Some prospective employees would have no qualms whatsoever about working with this population. Just be sure you feel good about the gender, age group, and backgrounds of the students.

Along with the mission statement, find out if the organization is Christian or has any religious affiliations. My wife and I are Baptists and have been for some time. When we were looking into various facilities, we tried to be as flexible as possible. We had an interview with a secular boarding school in Pennsylvania. We were excited at first about the prospect of working there, but as the interview progressed, the subject of church came up. Even though they did not have a problem with us going to church while on duty, they did not want us to require the students to go to church. My wife and I did not understand at all how we could go to church while at the same time not require the students to go to church. Were we just going to let the students run amuck while we worshipped? A different denomination can also cause personal strife. Dark Hills, the place where my wife and I worked, was a Presbyterian home. We were told by the director that it shouldn't pose a problem since Baptists and Presbyterians were so similar. Both of us learned the hard way that it did pose a problem, since the modes of worship and the doctrines differed greatly. One of my colleagues at Dark Hills was so disturbed by the doctrinal differences, that it was one of his reasons for leaving. Organizations labeled non-denominational are a fairly safe bet. If you do decide to work at a facility of a different denomination, find out what their policy is about attending a different style of church on your time off. How controlling are they about your worship? Find out ahead of time before you pursue that job opening.

Discipline is also a major thing to look into. Albeit overseas programs can be a wonderful experience for those who decide to go that route, many of these American based organizations can be much more austere in their discipline practices. When I was overseas, there was a set of house parents that came down with their six-year-old son. Everything seemed to be going well for the family until one of the students in their house had to see one of the administrators for disciplinary reasons. Not only were they appalled with the corporal punishment the student received, they went as far as to try to report the school to the American authorities for abuse. Though the school's method of discipline was acceptable by legal standards, it was apparent that the house parents did not realize what kind of program it was. It's also important to investigate whether or not you will be required to do any kind of restraints or physical intervention. Even though all programs provide their staff with training in this area, I personally did not feel comfortable with doing any kind of physical intervention. First of all, I'm not a physical person and do not have the physique of someone like Vin Diesel. I can honestly tell you that if I was required to take down a 200 pound, 17-year-old boy who, let's say, was on a wrestling team in high school, I don't know how it would turn out. There are those who may feel comfortable, even prefer, that kind of physical interaction. I also don't like aggressive physical intervention because in my experience, it has seldom been an effective tool. If a program has to frequently result in this kind of tactic with the same students, they really need to examine the clientele they are accepting. Either that or they need to examine their discipline policies.

Couples with children also need to do some examining of their own. I will say that in all honesty house parenting is not the type of career that married couples should pursue. (I will explain why at a later time.) Nevertheless, if you have a child and still feel the call of house parenting, be sure to find out if the program allows children and how many children you are allowed to have. When I was first looking into different facilities, there was an organization in the Southwest that looked very promising. When they told me that they did not hire staff with children younger than five years old, I slammed the receiver down in indignation. Later, I realized that that particular company actually did me a great favor in telling me ahead of time. Since it seemed like an unsafe and rowdy place to work, I was actually thankful we did not pursue that job (My apologies to the receptionist I slammed the receiver down on). Another organization I interviewed for only allowed one child per couple due to the number of young people they were allowed to have in their living quarters. Other organizations may require you to discipline and treat your child in the same manner you discipline the other students. In my opinion, how I discipline my child should be determined by my wife and I and not by any outside entity.

In conclusion, find out as much as you can about the organization as you can. If things are unclear from the web sites and literature, call them up and ask questions. Most receptionists are more than happy to answer any questions or address any concerns you may have. Talk with your spouse and family about the organization and by all means get their input. Don't waste your time filling out lengthy applications to places that don't have an immediate interest in you or do not sound like a place you would want to work.

APPLICATIONS AND INITIAL INTERVIEWS

There's not too much to say about the application process that would not pertain to applying to any other job like Wal-mart or any other store at your nearest shopping mall. One of the main differences is that house parent applications are significantly longer and more personal. Some applications require you to write essays about everything from your spiritual upbringing to your philosophy on discipline. Many can be filled out on line and sent right to the prospective employer. Others require you to take a multiple choice test, giving you various scenarios and choices on how you would deal with them. It is interesting to note that many major retail stores' applications are becoming increasingly longer and require you to do many of the same things. These kinds of assessments may be useful for the company, but I find these tests to be more of a nuisance and a waste of time. Whenever I had to take these things I found that I was answering the questions from the perspective of giving the prospective employer the answers they want to hear instead of answering the questions objectively. If you are applying to a Christian organization, it may be a good idea to write your testimony in essay form, since some places ask for one. Some places even require a photograph to be included with the application. Due to the sheer length of these applications, this is why you only want to fill out applications for companies that are hiring.

It is also helpful to obtain some kind of manual and job description. If you are able to get one, be sure it is relevant and up to date. Before going overseas to my teaching job, they mailed me a manual that was nearly ten years old. In between the time the manual was written and when I went down, significant changes were made to both the job description and the living conditions. Although I was determined to make my new job work, I could see where it might have filled other prospective staff with dread. Updated information is also important for web sites. Organizations should always be looking for ways to make their information and literature more appealing to soon-to-be staff and students alike.

Some programs will even send supplemental information in the form of DVDs. An advantage to these is you are able to actually get an accurate look at the campus without actually having to go there. Representatives, workers, and perhaps even some of the students may actually get an opportunity to explain the program in such a way that a pamphlet may not explain. You also get a better understanding about everyday life that you wouldn't otherwise be able to see in just one afternoon interview. Although a DVD does not guarantee a successful program, it does show two things. First of all, it gives you a general feel for the organization and their positive characteristics. Secondly, most organizations that put the effort toward making videos care about what kind of image they are trying to convey to the rest of the world.

Once the application is sent in, check back every few days if no one gets in contact with you. You never know if your application was lost in the mail or if it is sitting on the wrong person's desk. It also shows the prospective employer that you are genuinely interested in the position. It's not a good idea to call too frequently, otherwise you may come across as too pushy and irritating. Once they acknowledge its presence, leave it up to them to schedule any kind of interview. If they don't get back to you, chances are they aren't interested. One time my wife and I looked into a house parenting position on the east coast. The human resource department of the organization said there was an opening and they were interested in flying us out for an interview. The girl we talked to said that all she had to do was get the final go-ahead from the supervisors and she would call us back at the end of the day. Not only did she not call us back when she said she would, nobody answered the human resource extension whatsoever nor did they return any of my calls. I even called for several weeks afterward to find out what happened to our arrangement and sure enough, no one picked up or returned our messages. As heartbreaking as it was, we came to the conclusion that if that was the way the organization treated prospective staff members, the disregard for their staff could be even worse.

The majority of programs require you to fill out the application before they set up an initial interview. There was one place that set up the telephone interview before we filled out the application. The problem I had with this scenario was not the fact that we did not get the job, the organization required us to fill out the lengthy application and then they told us we would not be right for the job due to having a child less than a year old, which we were upfront with them within the first few minutes of the near hour and a half phone interview. If the organization was not sure if they wanted to hire us based on the interview, they should have waited to send us the application until they knew we were the right ones. The frustration of not getting the job was compounded by the time we wasted filling out the application.

Most programs will set up a primary telephone interview before inviting you out to tour their facilities. This is an excellent opportunity to not only get a feel for the program, but to also give you a chance to ask specific questions that the supplemental information did not address in detail. It is always a good idea to have a list of questions ready before the interview starts and to have it handy as you are interviewing. That way you don't beat yourself up if you forget to ask it. If you do forget and they set up a follow-up interview, you can always ask it when you are there.

During the interview, the director or the human resource representative will dazzle you with the history of their organization and the wonderful work they are doing with their clientele. They will make it sound like it is the best place in the whole world to work; it could be a horrible organization with more flaws than strengths, but obviously they would never tell you that. This is why you need to have those questions handy. Find out what kind of structure or daily schedule the students adhere to. Some organizations are taken back by this question and tell you that is up to the individual house parent to create the structure. One organization was somewhat slighted by this question and even responded sarcastically. This response is totally unacceptable, especially to new house parents who may not have the experience to know how to achieve this goal. In fact, we turned down a boarding school position in Texas because of this issue. (The importance of a schedule will be discussed in a later chapter.) Ask them about things like turnover rate of house parents or the financial soundness of the organization. A supervisor of mine moved halfway across the United States from Arizona to accept a department head position only to find out that the school was in dire financial straits. These are only a couple of the issues to address and there are many others, like visitation policies, time off, and any other special needs you or your spouse might have.

One question to avoid is asking about the success rate of the school. This is a totally useless question, in my opinion, because it is like asking a politician if he is honest. In the facilities' minds, the success rate is always much higher than it actually is. The CEO of a company I worked for would frequently tell people who asked him this question that the success rate of his company was one hundred percent because no student went through his program unchanged. A second issue I have with this question is that it is way too ambiguous. How does one gauge success? Vocational? Social? Spiritual? If it is a Christian organization you would think that spiritual success would be determined by whether or not the students convert to Christianity. However, if a student becomes a Christian in the program and then is given a jail sentence for a crime he committed, is the organization still successful? Yet another thing to consider is how schools determine "success rate" data. In the fifteen or so years I worked in a residential setting, I have found that the majority of the students do not keep in touch with the school once they leave. With the advent of Facebook and other internet connections however, communication in this area has been much more successful.

During any time of the application and interview process, it is always important to keep an open mind. If during any point of these processes something does not feel right, chances are your intuition is correct. My wife and I have turned down several prospective jobs due to the responses we received and the literature we read. Depending on where the position is, making arrangements to go out for a secondary interview can be quite an investment in time and money. Going out for a secondary interview to an organization you don't feel sure about would not be wise. If you are unemployed or really need to accept a job as soon as possible, it is easy to accept any position that comes along. Sadly, there is no preventing any company from stretching the truth or even lying during any of the process. Knowing the general pitfalls of any residential facility and how to look for them is the most important thing not only in your search but in your success.

THE SECONDARY INTERVIEW

The secondary interview is perhaps the most pivotal point in the whole house parenting search. There are many things to be on the lookout for and to talk about before making the crucial decision whether or not to work for the prospective organization. Whatever your observations, keep an open mind and stay objective. Don't be overtaken by desperation, thinking that if you don't get the job, you don't know what you'll do. Just remember that it's better to be honest and be turned down than to be hired and regret each day you work there.

It is paramount that you do not give the prospective employer the benefit of the doubt. As mentioned in the previous chapter, companies will try to dazzle you with promises and impressive information. Always be suspicious about things that don't look right or add up as this might be an indicator of bigger problems to come. Prospective employers are going to be very critical of you, so in return you should be somewhat critical of them. I'm not trying to say that every organization and boarding school is corrupt or deceptive, but it becomes more of a challenge to find potential problems when schools put on an upbeat presentation.

Whether you fly in or drive there; be aware of the setting of the school. More times than not, you will have to drive through some kind of town before reaching your final destination. Make note of the size of the surrounding community and how far away it is from where you work. When my wife and I flew east to interview for a job at a boarding school, we noticed how small and impoverished the town was as well as the relatively long distance it was from the school. I could foresee the inconvenience and hassle of having to drive into town, especially during inclement weather. There also did not seem like there would be much to do on our time off or if we ever decided to go somewhere with the students during a free day. What made matters worse was the fact that the house we would have been working at would have been nearly fifty miles away from the main campus. Since the administration lived closer to the central campus, it would take them nearly an hour for them to come out to the house should there ever be a disciplinary crisis.

Once you get to the main campus, observe the number and the conditions of the cottages and buildings. The first thing I noticed when we arrived at Dark Hills Academy was the surprisingly small size of the campus. When I looked at their web site and during the initial interview, I was told that there was going to be a mass expansion of the campus and several buildings erected, including all new cottages, a new school, and a new gymnasium. None of these buildings were even started being built and the campus just had three shabby looking cottages, a gymnasium, and a couple of office building. I am not opposed to small campuses, but there were two issues that bothered me. First of all, this organization bragged about being over one hundred years old and steeped in local history and cultural heritage. Even though they had a couple of impressive historic landmarks, all they had to show since its origin is a few worn-out looking buildings. Secondly, I was wondering where all of these new buildings were. I was aware that they hadn't started any of the construction yet, but there was no sign whatsoever that anything had even started. The only thing that was even remotely new was a half-sized basketball court that was being put in the day we interviewed. This issue will be brought up at a later time to illustrate the gross mismanagement and crooked practices of the aforementioned organization.

Other campuses we visited were impressive in size and well maintained. The landscaping was orderly, the houses looked clean on the outside, and there was ample room for several cottages to do outside activities. A clean campus with well maintained houses is an indication of how much they care about the image they are trying to portray to the students, employees, and the surrounding community. A school may say that they care about a positive image, but the tell-tale sign of this image is how pleasant the environment looks. It may also be an indicator of the financial condition of the organization. Buildings that are not well maintained may reflect the lack of funds the facility has.

After you arrive, go to the main office and let the secretary know of your arrival. As you do, note how friendly and organized the staff is. At one boarding school in the Midwest we interviewed at, the front desk had absolutely no idea who we were and where we were supposed to go. It took office staff nearly a half an hour to find someone who could help us. Someone eventually met us and took us to where we were going to stay. Throughout our visit, which was an overnight stay, it seemed as though they were always looking for someone to take care of us or to tell us where we should go next. It even took fifteen minutes to get the administrative staff to meet with us and to find an office where we could conduct the interview. From my perspective, if a business was that disorganized and non-communicative to someone from the outside, I could have only imagined how it would have been for someone who worked there.

The secondary interview process is usually an all day affair, starting some time in the morning and ending in the afternoon or evening. During this time, the interviewer will give an extensive tour of the campus and everything associated with the organization. Keep a very close eye on the apartments and don't be afraid to ask about where you will be staying. Sometimes the apartment will be unavailable for viewing if someone else is currently living there. If this is the case, ask about the size, the number of rooms, and access to the apartment. The apartment we had at Dark Hills had no private access into the apartment, which meant that any time we went into our apartment, we had to pass into the student residence. One door of our apartment was a few feet into the kitchen area, but the outside door had a lock which we did not possess a key. The other door was all the way across the living room of the student living area. Other places were so small, that there would have been nowhere near enough room for our modest amount of furniture and belongings. With the lack of privacy and cramped living conditions, the living quarters in some organizations were reason enough for my wife and me to turn down those positions.

If the school is on campus, the interviewer should have no problem taking you on a tour of the school, or at least to make arrangements to visit with some of the students. In order to get a good feel for the school climate, you should have the opportunity to visit with any student you come across and ask them general questions. Don't ask them specific questions, as this might be taken as an invasion of privacy and poor taste. Some places even arrange for the prospective house parents to eat dinner at one of the cottages to observe the structure of one of the houses. When we interviewed at Dark Hills, the CEO would not let us observe any of the students or even talk to one of them. It made me wonder if there was something that they didn't want us to know. I understood the need for confidentiality, but there should have been no reason why we couldn't have had some sort of interaction.

It would also be prudent to talk to staff presently working there and get their perspective on the job. Of all the people to talk to, these are the ones you really want to listen to, especially if there are potential problems with the position. A friend and coworker at Dark Hills warned prospective house staff that it was not a good organization and that the position was teeming with problems. In talking with my friend after the incident, he felt the interviewees may have dismissed him as just a disgruntled employee who did not have a clear perspective. Even if the staff member or ex-staff member is biased and has utter contempt for the organization, there had to have been something to make him feel the way he does. If the staff member thoroughly enjoys working there, find out about some of the things he enjoys about his job. Get the current house parents' read on some of the students and some of the things they may do on weekends or during the evening when they get home from school.

When my wife and I went through the interview process, we brought our infant daughter along who became a toddler in later job opportunities, since we did not have the luxury of leaving her at a babysitter for an extended period. Whether or not she was a liability to our interviews I'll never be quite sure. Nevertheless, we felt like since we were going to be working as a family, we should interview as one as well. It was interesting to see the various responses to our daughter by the interviewers. For example, at Dark Hills Academy, the director took us out to lunch in his SUV. When we said we needed to strap our daughter's carrier car seat which required the base that was in our car, he said that we didn't need to do so. Not only was this a blatant disregard for her safety, it was also illegal. The human resource director at the children's home back East seemed easily annoyed when our daughter started getting cranky. Another children's home actually provided our daughter with toys to play with while we interviewed. We did not realize till after all of the interviews that how they regarded all of our family, including our child, could have been an indication of how they would have regarded us when or if we worked there.

Although meals and accommodations do not necessarily reflect upon how efficiently the organization runs, it does reflect the charity and character of those in leadership. Just about all interviewers will treat you to at least one meal, depending on the length of the interview process. Many of the schools even provided sleeping accommodations, whether it was at a hotel or in their own homes. Some places were hospitable enough to make us breakfast since we stayed at their home. Be gracious, but don't think that hospitality is directly related to good leadership. The director at Dark Hills was very gracious and social, but as I will show you later, he was a very bad leader.

During the interview itself, they will usually ask about your previous work experience, testimony (if they are a Christian organization) and philosophy, and possibly different scenarios. If you are currently employed, they may ask about your present employer and why you have the desire to leave your present job. They will definitely ask about any gaps in employment and what you see as your weaknesses. If you are interviewing with your spouse, avoid disagreeing with her openly as this might be seen as an inability to work together. At this time, be sure to ask any questions that were not answered at the primary interview. It may be a good idea to ask about salary if you still do not know what it is. How much you make can definitely determine whether the job is for you. If you are a teacher, ask about the kind of curriculum they use and the amount of flexibility that is allowed as a teacher. Other things to ask about if you do not know by that time would be time off policy, job description and benefits.

After the interview process, you will more than likely be processing the whole experience with your spouse, or at least doing quite a bit of thinking if you are a single staff member. Be honest with your feelings and impressions as this could make the difference between choosing the job or not. If you are single, talk to someone about it either by cell phone or when you get home. That way you can cut through the dazzling display and talk about the job at hand. Discuss things that might have bothered you as well as any potential problems or concerns. If you have to provide housing for yourself off campus, or if you have other outstanding loans or expenses, be sure you can afford to work there; if it's a job you really want, you may want to make out a budget. Really think and pray about the pending decision to make sure it is the right organization for you.

It usually takes a week or so for an organization to make a decision about hiring. Never assume that you have the job. There were at least two different interviews that my wife and I were almost positive we had the job due to the good feeling we had after the interview. Sadly, it ended in disappointment. If you don't hear back within a week after the interview, it may not hurt to call back and see if they came to any decision. If you receive a letter through standard mail, chances are they hired someone else, especially if they start the letter by thanking you for your application. If they wanted you to start as soon as possible, it would be unlikely they would send you something that would be as slow as a ground letter. If they are interested, they will either call you directly or send you an e-mail. Whatever the case, keep this in mind: God will put you in the place He wants you to be. There's an old cliché that says whenever He closes a door He opens a window. Don't be discouraged; keep applying. If you don't get any prospects after you apply for long periods of time, you may want to consider whether you really are being called into the field. After at least three failed interviews in a row, I felt like God was telling me to stop applying and seek employment elsewhere. Don't be disappointed and always be open to God's calling.

PART 2:
THE BEST OF TIMES

THE OVERSEAS EXPERIENCE

I was twenty-four years old and single when I went overseas to the Caribbean Islands to work at my first American boarding school. I knew absolutely nothing about the host country and spoke very little, if any, Spanish. What made matters worse was the fact that I arrived a week before the Christmas holiday, which made the airport an absolute madhouse. There were people everywhere with suitcases the size of piano cases, all waiting to have their bags inspected to enter the country. There was even a three man string band adding to the cultural flavor. The inspection process took a grotesque amount of time and I had no idea where I was going or even what I was doing there. The person who was scheduled to take me to the compound was not there to pick me up, and I was harassed by a pushy taxi driver whom I mistook as one of the workers who was supposed to take me to the compound.

Though the person who was supposed to pick me up finally showed up, and it all worked out in the end, I realize how many mistakes I made. First of all, I did little, if any, research on the host country. Even though there would have been no way to learn the language in the very short amount of time between when I was hired and when I flew down, it would have been beneficial to at least bought some kind of translator or book of common phrases in the native language. Flying down during a major holiday was also not a good idea, regardless of how desperate I was to start work. It also would have been a good idea to somehow communicate with the people picking me up concerning the time of my arrival.

Before I went overseas, the human resource person warned me several times about culture shock. Even though the school was American, it was based in a foreign country. Everything from how food was cooked to frequent blackouts was covered in the briefing. Even going to the bathroom and flushing toilet paper was something that wasn't something that could be taken for granted. Most people think that living overseas entailed either living in a grass hut or working on the beach. Shopping was also something that was nothing like in the United States. The novelty of being in a foreign country was exhilarating and not nearly as bad as I thought it was going to be. Nevertheless, the lack of American conveniences and more relaxed lifestyle was something that could be stressful at times.

Many staff members had a very difficult time being away from family and loved ones. There were at least three staff members I can think of off hand that suffered the entire time they were down there because they sorely missed family members and beaus. Consequently, they quit their post before their Christian service agreement was up (A Christian service agreement is a non-binding contract between the organization and youth care worker). Since I was unemployed for at least four months and living with my parents, going to a foreign country was a welcome change. Keep in mind at this point in time, the internet was not available for at least another two years, but now, in the age of texting and instant messaging, communication is not as much of an issue. If being away from family is going to be an issue or if you are in a dating relationship, going overseas, or even a long distance away, is not a good idea.

I also had the advantage of being single. As I mentioned earlier, if you are going to make any major changes, make sure your spouse is just as zealous about going as you are. There are going to be times when living overseas are going to be stressful. If your spouse's heart is not into being there, they are not going to be the support you may need. Not only that, you may spend a large amount of time trying to be an encouragement to your husband or wife who may resent being in the present situations. It was interesting to see how many of the house parents who came down to work were newly married and in their early to mid-twenties. Some organizations require the couples to be married a certain length of time since house parenting can be somewhat stressful on a marriage. Many of them stayed for their required time of two years and moved on, but a surprising number of couples stayed on for longer or transferred to another one of the campuses.

If you are single and work as a house parent, there are a different set of challenges you may face. First of all, you don't really have much of a choice of who your house father or house mother is going to be. Since you work very closely with your fellow house parent, it's imperative that you get along very well, or at least understand how the other one thinks. Most organizations will not hire single staff for this position because it is much easier to hire couples for the job as opposed to hiring individuals. Some organizations have what they call the group leader position, which is the person who watches the cottages while the house staff are off. Unlike a married couple, you do not have that intimate support when times get difficult. Since house parents work opposite shifts of everyone else, the only ones who are off with you are other house parents. If you are single, there really is no one else to interact with on your time off, except for other single house parents, who are more the exception more than the rule. When I was working in the student house overseas, there was no television to watch or no internet. Since I did not ride a motorcycle, I also had to stay on campus. Boredom does not seem like a major issue, but weeks upon weeks of it can really be a drain on your morale.

One of the things that single house staff, particularly men, have a temptation of doing is getting too intimately attached to the other single house staff. There is absolutely nothing wrong with staff members who want to connect relationally, but guys have a tendency to get the wrong idea about the females they are working with. They will sometimes confuse their roles as house staff and interpret it as a dating relationship. Once they find that the house mother is not interested in them socially, they tend to be disillusioned and even crushed. One time when I was working at the same boarding school in the United States, a house father quit without warning during the night because the house mother would not go out on a date with him. Although everybody seeks some level of connection to other human beings, single female house staff tend to be more mission driven and less interested in dating relationships than single male house staff. Dating someone you work with in the house may not be a good idea anyway; if the relationship does not work out, you will always have some kind of tension present when you work with the person you broke up with.

It is true that being overseas created quite a bit of culture shock. The mundane things in everyday life from going shopping to having steady electricity are sorely missed once they are not present. However, any time somebody was going through a difficult time overseas, administration attributed it to having culture shock. Although culture shock was prevalent, what I struggled with most was what I call program shock. When you live in the place where you work, you never really feel like you can get away. Some staff knew enough Spanish to go out into the community and interact with the natives. Since I wasn't fluent enough in Spanish, the majority of my time was spent with the other staff I worked with. When I first went down, I did not feel like I connected to the other staff in a way I should have. Within three months of being down in the Caribbean, I wanted to go home. To make matters worse, the other guys in the staff house and I did not get along. We eventually worked out our differences, and I ended up staying for quite a while longer. Another staff member I worked with had terrible boundaries and wild mood swings. Working in a closely knit setting requires building strong relationships, tolerance, boundary setting, and belief in the work you do.

Whenever you have people living in a small community, there is a tendency for certain staff members to be bullies. Although they may not threaten to beat you up on the playground, they are usually very loud and aggressive in nature. They act like administrators by making demands and threatening to get you into trouble, but in actuality, they are nothing more than your peers. They also frequently question decisions you make and are usually avoidant of social situations. These kinds of staff members tend to be demeaning, harsh, and sometimes even abusive toward the students in their care. What makes these people dangerous is how their aggression is embraced by administrators; once that happens, most anything these bullies say is believed and accountability goes out the window. To make matters worse, these people will even vie for administrative positions and may even get it. The harsher the bullying, the more the quality and integrity of the program will be jeopardized. Some less aggressive staff members may even befriend these bullies to avoid getting in their way. The best way to deal with bullies is to avoid them altogether. If you have to work with them directly, keep your professionalism up and don't take what they say or do personally. If they have a problem with your work, talk to them about it, but don't argue with them. Admit when you make mistakes, as that tends to diffuse their bullying somewhat. If it gets too out of hand, talk to your direct supervisor and be very matter-of-fact about incidents; avoid generalizations and labeling. Administrative bullies will be addressed later in the writing.

Above all, take advantage of your overseas experience. Take time off to tour various parts of the country. Don't let inconveniences and differences in their culture frustrate you. Most of the time, Americans are viewed as impatient and pushy because they expect things to run as efficiently as they do in the United States. Even things like automobile repairs and utility installation take significantly longer in foreign countries. Remember that you are a guest in the country you are living in, so observe traditions and customs without compromising your personal beliefs. Women are not viewed as equals in many countries and in some cases, are even viewed as objects of desire. It is a good idea for women to go out either in groups or with a man, never alone. Always remember that a poorly run program does not necessarily reflect a poorly run country.

EMOTIONAL COOKIES

Cookies and desserts by far have to be one of the most beloved of all foods. Whenever I go home to visit, one of the things my mother does is bake cookies. Two of my favorite types of cookies that she bakes are chocolate chip cookies and date stuffed oatmeal cookies. There is just something about them that make me feel good about being home and make me feel unconditionally loved and appreciated. These kinds of comfort foods provide instant pleasure and gratification, though they are high in calories and low in nutritional value. The richer or larger the dessert or cookie, the greater pleasure it brings. One of the things my wife did when she was a house mother was make desserts and snacks for when the students came home from school. The students' favorite desserts were either her banana pudding or her no-bake cookies. She could have bought pre-packaged cookies, but there was more of a display of love and care for the students making things homemade, especially for those who were not blessed with loving mothers or home-cooked meals.

When I started working at Bright Meadows Academy overseas, I was introduced to quite a bit of jargon I had never heard before. One of these odd terms was "emotional cookies." Emotional cookies are displays of unconditional love and affection shown toward another person, whether it be toward your spouse, your own children, or the students you work with. It's a quick "feel good" solution, whether someone is hurt, sad, or depressed through use of kind words, gestures, or deeds. It can be anything from a quick word of encouragement to doing something kind or considerate. Usually emotional cookies are given without knowing, or even caring, about any negativity that the student was involved in. Its main objective is to make the person feel loved, understood, and accepted.

One of the roles of a house mother is to give these emotional cookies to the students. Where I worked at Bright Meadows, the house father ran the structure of the house and the house mother supported the house father, yet always gave unconditional love to the students, even when they were unlovable. Just as eating my mother's cookies filled me with comfort, the housemother's emotional cookies filled the students with comfort. It seems like in many troubled families, mothers run the family and the fathers are either non-existent, busy doing something else, or passive in child rearing. Mothers have become the ones who uphold the structure of the house instead of being the ones who are the understanding ones. When we think of the mother's traditional role in the family, we think of shows like <u>Leave It to Beaver</u> or <u>The Brady Bunch</u>. Most organizations want house mothers to be more of a supportive and nurturing role and the house father to be the one who controls the house.

The majority of the problems Bright Meadows had with their house parents were working within the confines of the roles. Instead of giving emotional cookies and being a support to the house father, they took on the discipline themselves and made the important decisions in the house. The students saw the house father as weak and the house mother as nasty and domineering. What made this especially bad was the fact that instead of showing the students how a healthy family dynamic worked, it was no different from what they might have observed at home. When confronted about this, house mothers complained that the house father either didn't observe the negative behavior, so they took matters into their own hands, or the house father didn't deal with it appropriately. House fathers and house mothers like this usually grew up in a family setting where the mother was the leader of the family and continued in these roles well into adulthood. The key to successful house parenting is to overcome these negative roles and to work within the roles laid out by the organization.

Within boarding schools and residential facilities, there is a very strong temptation to give excessive amounts of emotional cookies. There are several reasons for this. First of all, some students, especially the younger ones, are viewed as cute and helpless by their house staff. It may bring out excessive feelings of adoration and protection, like the kind of coddling a doting grandmother may give a sobbing grandchild. Students who are older, more mature, and higher functioning in behavior are also prone to get too much attention from house staff. Even though these students may look like adults and express themselves in a more adult manner, staff forget that they are still students in the program with much to learn. Another reason for giving excessive emotional cookies is what I like to call the Pygmalion complex. In Greek mythology, Pygmalion was a sculptor who created a statue of a beautiful woman. When the goddess Aphrodite brought the statue to life, the sculptor fell in love with his creation. As teachers and house parents, we may put a tremendous amount of time and effort into very needy students. When they improve with the help we provide, pride has a tendency to cloud our judgment. We see ourselves as miracle workers and feel a passionate need to protect these students from harm or failure. Staff members who have weak relationships with other staff members also tend to subject themselves to these negative relationships.

It is natural to want close relationships and great influence with your students. Although giving some words of encouragement and unconditional love can be a good thing, students can develop a sense of entitlement and helplessness. Johnny was a ten-year-old who came to us very emotionally immature. His house parents loved on him more than the others, or so it appeared. When we were on duty, he was very manipulative and bossy; as soon as he was confronted about what he was doing, he would look at us with doleful, puppy dog eyes, hoping to evoke sympathy. Perhaps the house parents felt like the student could not succeed with other staff members or that other staff members were too harsh or unfair. When my wife and I were off duty, we presumed that Johnny was telling his regular house parents about his terrible his treatment was while we were on duty. The acquired helplessness is not necessarily limited to young children, either. Joel had been at Dark Hills Academy for nearly three years. He was an amiable student whom both the staff and students had tremendous respect for. He was an average student, but since he was so well loved by the teachers, the teachers had a tendency to do most of the work for him. Consequently, when he went to college for the first time, he dropped out after only two months and went back to Dark Hills.

Emotional cookies and preferential treatment can not only lead to entitlement, but also a sense of invincibility and infallibility. This is especially true for students who are spoiled by those in administration. Aiden was thirteen years old, but had been at Dark Hills for over four years. He became a sort of poster child for the program, since his face was on most advertising for Dark Hills Academy. He could be very charming and friendly, but he also had a very mean and cold side. Administration thought very highly of Aiden and allowed him to come to the office whenever he wanted to. If he desired something or wanted to complain about something, it was nothing for him to ask to talk to the administrator. He was also very aware of confidential information, like events that were not yet posted and what staff were fired and why. In the year and a half we were there, we watched Aiden become more manipulative toward staff and more of a bully toward his peers. A fellow house father and I would joke that the reason why Aiden wasn't held accountable for his actions was that Dark Hills did not want to lose its poster child.

Older and higher functioning students are more prone to get preferential treatment as well. Curt came to Dark Hills with very few behavioral or academic issues. In fact, he came of his own accord and allowed the program to work for him. As a result, Mike, the homelife director at Dark Hills, frequently called Curt "his favorite" and flaunted this fact in front of the other students. Although Curt was well liked and respected by the students, Mike was not. Moreover, Mike did not interact with the other students half as much as he did with Curt. Needless to say Mike's scope of influence was very limited and he was eventually let go for undisclosed reasons. It is ironic that the lower functioning and more unlovable students really need the emotional cookies and encouragement, but actually get less than students who are likeable and higher achieving.

Staff members who show favoritism are also affected as well as their professionalism. Since teachers and youth care workers usually spend more time with the students in a boarding school, there is a tendency to form closer relationships. As a rule, troubled youth benefit greatly from this kind of setting, but staff members who give too much grace and emotional cookies are not as objective when they deal with their students. While showing favoritism to a select few or toward just one, they tend to be harsher and stricter toward the other students, especially toward those that show any kind of negativity toward their chosen student. Grades and behavioral points are often inflated with excessively glowing reviews about the student's progress. This may seriously distort tracking the student's progress if all they get are good comments with no room for improvement. When confronted about this, staff members vehemently deny any signs of favoritism and justify the need to coddle the student. They may also question other staff members who try to hold their student accountable or even punish their student.

Greg was a student who came from a broken family. His mother all but abandoned him and his father did not show much compassion for him either. As a young teenager, Greg started acting out in school and getting into fights. His father placed him at Dark Hills in a desperate attempt to turn the boy's life around. Once he was placed, however, Greg's father also severed communication with him. Since he had no family and no prospects for a future, the director of Dark Hills embraced Greg as a son and began to give him special privileges. This preferential treatment only exacerbated Greg's personal issues; toward the end of his stay, he became more arrogant, insolent, and argumentative with the authority figures around him, including the director himself. He was also overly aggressive and abusive toward the other students. It was obvious that the director was blinded by his concern and well being, but he insisted that he knew exactly what he was doing concerning Greg. Greg was eventually expelled for fighting at his vocational school and insubordination and ended up living on the streets in town.

If unchecked, relationships like these have the potential to get out of hand, causing the relationship to take on the characteristics of an addiction. Thoughts about the favored student can turn obsessive and personal emotions may become directly affected by the students' progress. The staff member will want to spend as much time around their favorite student as possible. Whether it be through extra privileges and trips off campus, superfluous amounts of time spent with the student is definitely a red flag. They may even find themselves attracted to the student, crossing professional and ethical boundaries. Once this happens, staff members may even be tempted to become physically involved with the student. Not only does this create legal headaches for the staff member, the organization may find themselves liable for the indiscretions of the staff member. I have known staff members to be fired and even be arrested for sexual misconduct, ruining their career as a youth care worker forever.

Though giving excessive emotional cookies will seldom go this far, it definitely affects the integrity of the staff member. There are certain signs to look for to see whether or not poor boundaries exist between staff and students. One of the most obvious things to look for is the amount of time and effort a staff member may put into a particular student or the extra amount of activities the staff member spends with the student. Another thing to look for is how the teacher or worker in question responds to positive criticism about the special student. If it seems like the staff member never points out negative behavior and becomes defensive when negative things are pointed out, this is not a good sign. Excessive hugging, wrestling, touching, and even joking around are also dangerous things; this may indicate personal boundaries are crossed, particularly if the staff member is male. Youth care workers or administrators who have poor relationships with peers and are harsh with the other students may also be an indication of poor boundaries.

Nobody ever wants to rashly accuse another staff member of favoritism or poor boundaries. However, there are some things that you can do to help the situation. The first thing to do is get to know the staff member to understand his way of thinking. Sometimes people are just really friendly by nature and give emotional cookies to most everybody. Always be objective and professional whenever giving positive and negative input about the students. If the other staff member becomes defensive, ask them to help you understand why they may feel this way. Some people are just hypersensitive about how you talk about the students, and may not necessarily be showing favoritism. If it is a serious enough concern and you have a close enough relationship with the staff member in question, you may want to lovingly confront them. If it is still a concern, you may want to talk to your direct supervisor about it. Unfortunately, if it is the head of the organization, there's really not much you can do about it. As with anything, emotional cookies can be effective if used in moderation. However, Jesus loves us unconditionally, yet holds us to a high standard of excellence. As Proverbs 27:5 says, "Open rebuke is better than secret love."

LEAVING THE TEACHING
TO TEACHERS

One of the biggest drawing cards to boarding schools is the individualized education the students receive. The majority of the students in boarding schools have had some kind of academic dysfunction or disability at their schools back home. In desperation, parents look for their child's academic limitations to be addressed in a way that boarding schools advertise. The biggest advantage that these kinds of institutions offer is the low student to staff ratio, which provides the students with more one-on-one interaction with teachers. It is without question that many public school classrooms are overcrowded and getting worse every year. As a result, student performance is suffering greatly. Students are also able to work ahead at residential schools in such a way they might not have been able to at their school back home.

When I taught at the Caribbean boarding school, I enjoyed the lack of disciplinary problems that I had to deal with because the program's structure was able to deal with these issues. I was also able to teach classes that I really didn't have training in but thoroughly enjoyed, like English literature and algebra. When I worked with students on an individual basis, I not only felt like I was helping them understand the material more effectively, but that I was building trust and a strong bond with my students that I would never have been able to do working at a public school. We were also able to customize the classes to the students' needs much more effectively and to start them whenever they were ready instead of having to wait for the next year or semester to begin.

A mixed blessing associated with teaching at a small Christian school is the different academic demands that may be put on a teacher. Even though a teacher might be hired to be a math teacher, he might also be called upon to teach another class, like English or science. Since I had several interests in topics other than science, teaching classes like English or music appreciation was both a challenge and a joy. Other classes were not as easy, like advanced math or government. Independent study classes usually just involved looking at an answer key whenever a student needed help with a question or for grading purposes. However, if the question was beyond the understanding of the teacher, it sometimes required further research or for the student to understand the teacher's limitations.

At first, individualized tutoring seemed like the ideal way to see to the students' educational issues. However, the longer I worked at the Caribbean program, the more I began to see other issues arise. The biggest issue I saw was providing instructional help to all of the students who needed it in a timely fashion. Math was definitely one class that the majority of the students were unable to do without the frequent aid of the teacher. Consequently, there were so many students signed up to see the math teacher, there was no conceivable way the math teacher was able to see all of the students in need in an allocated amount of time. Secondly, the paperwork and records for recording grades seemed complicated and overwhelming. In fact, when I was training to be a teacher at the Caribbean school, it took nearly a full week of training to know how to record grades using their system. It would make matters even worse if other teachers before you were not doing it properly. Since the program did not have a high teacher population, we were called upon frequently to either teach classes we knew next to nothing about or to tutor a large number of students. Although tutoring students individually was enjoyable, the longer I tutored, the more I felt like I was beginning to repeat myself. Sometimes I would find myself helping three different students in the same day on the same assignment.

When I started teaching twenty or so years ago in the Caribbean program, the students were best classified as high potential / low achieving students. In other words, they had the capability to do well in school, but they just chose to do poorly. As time went on, however, the student potential began to take a downturn. By the mid-2000s, many of the students were unable to work individually on assignments like they were able to when I first started. Remedial classes had to be developed and different textbooks had to be purchased to better facilitate the wide range of academic disabilities. Several students had to have a teacher right by their side in order to understand and finish assignments. With a low teacher population, it would make it nearly impossible to help the students finish their work. Students in the 1990s might have had behavioral issues, but there was still an inner drive to do well in all aspects of life, including in school. Fifteen years on, I have found the students lack that inner drive to do well and as a result, they are not accomplishing as much as they used to.

What I felt the school needed were more classes where students worked as a group. My last year at the Caribbean school was spent designing actual classes for all of the students and me to meet together and talk about any problems on the homework. Since I was a biology teacher as well, I designed lab activities for the students to do. This made answering student questions significantly easier because I did not have to repeat myself. When I transferred to the American campus of Bright Meadows Academy, my job title was education department head. The first thing I noticed was how many students were behind schedule and not getting done with classes in a timely fashion. One of my missions in my managerial role was to rectify many of the problems I saw in the students' learning. Since students benefited greatly from learning in a group, I worked with many of the teachers, particularly the math teachers since students struggled the most in math classes, to have effective learning and more productive students. Group classes were by no means new, but they proved to be very effectual.

With a new idea that seemed to show promise of success, one would think that it would be a welcome change to an old routine. Although many teachers and administrators praised the new system, it was by no means a totally welcome system by everybody, particularly with the directors of the programs. Since many, if not all, of them did not have a background in education, they did not understand the new way of teaching whatsoever. Moreover, the directors had been at the school for several years and were used to the old way of doing things. Allan, one of the directors, told me that they would be willing to make necessary changes, but they still wanted to keep the old way of doing things. To me, this was like buying a car and not being able to drive it. Doing both systems simultaneously was just not going to work. After several months of disagreements and debates over what was going to be an acceptable compromise, the teachers and directors were able to settle on a plan that was going to help the students and to accommodate the teachers to doing a more effective job.

There are two things that all programs will say about their education department. The first one is that they provide a "quality education." To me, this is as trite of an expression as a "high success rate." No school would ever admit to having poor quality education, unless they wanted to turn away prospective staff and students. The issue is really accurately defining what is meant by "quality education." High grades? Independent learning? Life long learners? The other thing that all programs will say about their schools is the fact that they are successful in teaching kids where public schools fail. When I first started working at Bright Meadows, this was indeed the case. However, as the years progressed, students actually started falling way behind. Betty, one of our more experienced teachers, refused to advertise this fact because she felt it was a false claim. If a school is truly going to brag about helping students catch up with their school work and assisting them in working ahead, it has to be constantly evaluating and monitoring student progress and making changes when necessary.

So what makes a successful boarding school? In my experience, a successful boarding school allows the teachers enough flexibility to help students do their best, whether it is a variety of curricula or working with every student effectively. Successful boarding schools also have staff that truly care about their students and hold them accountable. I've known teachers openly admit they don't like teaching, like the one teacher I mentioned at the beginning of the book. Apathy and indifference do not belong in any school. Most importantly, since students are always changing, schools must meet the challenges to assist students and to help them achieve their best.

OFFENSES AND BLAME

Most boarding schools, if not all of them, work with students with special needs. Some of these needs entail teaching them proper moral and ethical decision making. Since these areas are seriously lacking in their lives, it is vital as a youth care worker, regardless of position, to watch these students scrupulously. Although you may have love and compassion for this group, they know how to manipulate, cheat, and commit inappropriate behavior behind your back, and even under your nose. Some of them may even be prone to violence and criminal behaviors, such as stealing and sexual offending. Whatever the case, the majority of these students would be classified as high risk, meaning that they could become a danger to themselves, others, and personal property.

A good program will brief the child care staff of relevant background issues or supervisory concerns. For example, if a house parent is made aware that the child has theft issues, that house parent will know not to allow this student to walk through any kind of store unsupervised. If a house parent is aware of the fact that a student is a sex offender, they will definitely want to be vigilant when that student is around younger students and especially their own children, if they have any. Even if a student has a history of pornography use, it is something to be knowledgeable of to help monitor the child's behavior. There have been countless times that I had wished I was made aware of these facts before an incident related to a past issue occurred.

The majority of acute behavioral and disciplinary issues tend to happen after the set bedtime. These could include anything from smoking and substance abuse, to physical assault, to sexual acting out (individual schools may have their own policies on private masturbation). When a house parent goes on duty, it is a good idea to find out who the on-call administrator is. The on-call administrator is the one the youth care workers calls if there is any severe behavioral issue to take care of. When I was a house father, it was my job to respond to any noises that I might have heard during the night. One place I worked at required me to sleep with a baby monitor in my sleeping quarters and with the microphone placed in the student dormitory. These kinds of students are so clever and wily, most of them figure out a way to commit their inappropriate acts without the house parents even knowing. Some places also have motion detectors and door alarms for students who are runaway risks.

The biggest problem I've seen with discipline is when students act out in public. I've had students steal from retail stores even in my proximity. I've also had students who exhibit physical and verbal acts of aggression, including shouting, pushing, and even picking fights. When this happens, you feel foolish, helpless, or incompetent as a youth care worker. When my wife and I worked as house parents at Dark Hills, we seldom took the students out because they were unable to act appropriately at home. Students frequently complained about not going out and "doing something fun"; in response, I told them point blank that I didn't trust them and that if they acted better that we would take them somewhere.

You can always tell what kind of empathy a program has for its staff by taking a look at how they deal with major student disciplinary issues. An effective school may address any supervisory flaws with the staff member, yet have enough understanding that the same thing could have happened to any staff member. When I was on runaway watch, I turned my back for a minute only to have the student run out the door and into the woods in the middle of the night. Even though it was glaringly obvious I was to blame, no blame was cast and all the staff members worked together to apprehend the runaway. I have let my guard down more times than I care to admit only to be taken advantage of by a crafty and opportunistic student. Bright Meadows seemed to understand that their staff members were only human. Dark Hills, on the other hand, punished a staff member because one of the students they were supervising stole an item from a department store. The student received nothing more than a mild scolding and was required to wear a white wrist band as a reminder of his offense. However, the staff member was demoted to relief house staff. At another residential facility I worked at for a very short time, a 300+ pound client was ready to attack me because I was protecting another client's privacy. The administrators ruled it my fault because the client knew I was afraid of him and responded by decreasing my hours.

For behaviors that are more overt, it is important to have an administrator readily available. Most directors do not like regular house staff taking potentially physical matters into their own hands for liability reasons. However, there have been countless times that administrators were nowhere to be found in times of crisis. One time a student refused to get out of the shower after being in there for over twenty minutes. When I opened the door to the bathroom, the student started shouting uncontrollably. Sadly, there were no administrators to be found to help me deal with the situation. Not only was this an inconvenience, it could have also been dangerous If this situation ever occurs to you, either call an administrator who is not on duty or call on another staff member. If any supervisor has a problem with this, explain to them that the person who was supposed to be on call was not available for assistance. Minor issues like disrespect probably don't merit a telephone call to an administrator; however, non-compliance is something that should be reported. Other administrators see calling the on-call person as sign of incompetence or weakness. This fallacy only worsens feelings of helplessness and frustration on the staff member's part.

An effective program should rarely fault the staff members for students' negative behaviors. There are times, however, that house parents lose their tempers and don't respond properly to situations, which will cause students to react negatively. If you realize that you are to blame for the crisis, I see no weakness in apologizing to the student for what you said or did wrong. Just remember not to blame yourself too much in order to avert outbursts. Calling administration for problems should never be a poor reflection of the house staff; if anything, it's a reflection on the program itself. Either administrators aren't supporting the staff like they should, they are accepting students they are unable to handle, or there is not enough training taking place. House staff crying "wolf" is not a good thing, either. This will definitely give you a bad reputation with not only the administrators, but with the other students as well.

Don't be deceived by any student's pleasantries; remember that the students are there for a reason. Granted, not all students are going to be thieves or hooligans, but they are all going to need intensive supervision in some way, shape, or form. What makes house parenting so difficult is that you can't let your guard down for a minute. Even if a students tells you they are "allowed to do this", always check to make sure with your supervisor. Trust is something that needs to be earned and should never be taken for granted.

THE TWO IMPORTANT THINGS

As I mentioned earlier, house parenting is not a lucrative profession. Nevertheless, I worked at Bright Meadows Academy for close to twenty years and had every intention of working there longer. So what was it that kept me working there for so long? There were actually two things: relationships and experience.

When I first started working as a teacher, I was very ineffective and most of the classroom experiences I had were a disaster. Although I student taught and already taught one year at a Christian school, I didn't feel like I was growing as a teacher; I put in enough man hours, but I seriously lacked experience. Bright Meadows not only taught me how to be an effective teacher, they also taught me how to effectively deal with staff and students alike. Many organizations that utilize the house parent model seem to attract young, idealistic workers and couples who lack true child care experience. Effective employers are willing to work with these people to develop child care skills and make them better youth care workers.

Some institutions will even help pay for graduate studies. If it were not for Bright Meadows, I would never have been able to pay to complete my master's degree. The only stipulation was I had to stay beyond my two-year contract. For every month I stayed with Bright Meadows, they put one hundred dollars toward my graduate studies. Organizations should also be willing and able to send staff to relevant seminars and workshops. This kind of training embellishes the experience of child care and adds to the staff members' ability to deal with various situations. The only thing about seminars and workshops is the fact that they really needs to be practical. Too many times I attended yearly workshops that either didn't relate to what I did at Bright Meadows or were a repetition of the previous year. They can be also very time consuming, depending on the length of the conference.

The other thing that staff should walk away with from an effective youth care facility is relationships. If a facility is successful in teaching students how to form relationships, it will definitely be infectious for all those who work for the organization. I have to confess that before going to Bright Meadows, I seriously lacked the skills to form close relationships. I would also mistake effective teaching to forming peer-like relationships with the students. This faulty reasoning caused me to be ineffectual as a teacher. The main thing that Bright Meadows taught students was how to have relationships with appropriate boundaries. In order to teach students this, one needs to learn these lessons as well. There were more than a couple of times I was confronted by the director that my relationships with staff were superficial and the "friendships" I had with the students were not appropriate because I treated them more like equals. Although at the time I found these confrontations presumptuous, I found them a harsh wake up call.

The relationships I formed at Bright Meadows were some of the closest relationships I have to this day. I feel nothing but gratitude toward the director because he always showed concern for me and his staff. I now know the difference between healthy relationships and poor boundaries between staff and students. Due to the wonder of Facebook, I still keep in touch several of my ex-students and ex-coworkers. Many of my ex-coworkers are still an integral part of my life and offer me council and advice.

Relationships also hold supervisors accountable to treating their subordinates with consideration and respect. If supervisors respect their staff in a relational way, they will discreetly and lovingly offer criticism that is helpful and edifying. Bosses that isolate themselves from their staff and openly rebuke their subordinates in front of others, it is obvious that relationships do not really matter to them. This total disregard for the staff's feelings and self-respect has a tendency to set a negative climate for the entire organization.

The CEO of Bright Meadows used to remark frequently that the staff members grow just as much as the students do. As I look back on my experiences, the most effective residential facilities helped me grow and develop not only as a teacher and a youth care worker, but also as a human being. The desire to be a better person in a community that nurtures personal and professional development should be contagious with all those you work along side of. If an organization does not foster positive relationships and give you valuable experiences, it may not be the best place to work.

THE SAD DECISION TO LEAVE

With the amount of paperwork, the enormous amount of responsibility, and the intensive supervision, it goes without saying that working at a residential youth care facility is a very stressful job with a high degree of burnout. Even the early morning and late evening hours cause a tremendous amount of strain. As mentioned earlier, the average stay of a houseparent couple is about two years, depending on the quality of the facility. Teachers do not have as high a burnout rate because the hours are different and the responsibilities are not as rigorous. They are also able to go home away from the stresses of their job. Nevertheless, teaching at a residential school can cause stresses that are different from a regular public or private school. One of the biggest stressors of any facility can be working within the confines of the organization itself. Since the administration's responsibility is to keep consistent structure for the students, that means that flexibility for new ideas can be extremely limited. If the staff member does not agree with how things are run and realize they can do very little to change it, many times there is no choice but to leave. Of course, every ex-staff member has their own personal reasons for leaving.

Most of the house parents who start working at a residential facility are spiritually active couples who are very flexible to where God is leading them. The range of age can be anywhere from early twenties to retirees in their mid-sixties. They are unafraid to pack up their belongings and move to that organization that shows a tremendous amount of promise. (Since relocation is a huge task, this is why I gave the warning at the beginning of the book to make sure it would be an organization that you would feel comfortable in.) Many of the new house parents did not have children initially, but I have found that quite a number of new recruits now have at least one child, like my wife and I did. Teachers, however, can be of various ages. The majority of them are local residents because they already have families with jobs elsewhere in the community.

When you start out as a house parent, you are less concerned about long-term goals and more concerned about making your current residential calling work. As time goes on, however, long-term goals seem to be more relevant. Couples may want to have another child or move into a house of their own. They may also want careers that are not going to be as stressful or that are more lucrative. These kinds of desires seriously conflict with the job of a youth care worker and cause the workers to make the decision to leave their once beloved position. The house parents may love their job and the students they work with and have a real calling to meet their needs, but the needs of the family will, and should, always come first. As a house parent, you realize that the house you live in is not your house, it's "their house", meaning that the house belongs to the organization and not you. The need for residential independence and a family identity outside the program becomes much too strong for couples who are growing in their relationship.

For a well run organization, the house parents may still have the desire to work, but they want to move away from working in the residential house. They may apply for administrative or teaching positions and decide to move off campus. Some facilities may graciously provide housing for these couples for a small monthly fee. Although it is significantly cheaper than renting or owning a house in the community, it is better for non-house parent couples to live off campus simply to get away from their work environment. There may also be less of a tendency to be called upon for additional responsibilities simply for being on campus. The more one can get away from work, the easier it is to be refreshed and have a new perspective on your job. House parents do not have this luxury because most, if not all, of them are required to live on campus.

House parents who remain in their initial calling is a rarity indeed. There are those who have enough tenacity to stay with what God has purposed in their life. Most of them, however, look at house parenting as a moment of transition in their lives and an opportunity to gain valuable experience in the areas of childcare and ministry. Some staff members are ex-students who are returning from whence they came to give back what the organization gave to them. It is interesting to note how many ex-students become counselors or youth care workers. Toward the end, the house staff may view their job as a tour of duty and literally count the days till they start something different. By this time, the house parents lose their effectiveness with the students and would be better off moving to another place or occupation.

As much as I loved Bright Meadows, there were several factors that attributed to my departure. First of all, many things changed when my daughter was born.

Since my wife and I could not afford child care and both of us needed to work, we needed to work opposite shifts to take care of our baby. It worked for a while, but I recognized that so much time apart was not healthy for our marriage because of the lack of communication. Secondly, the money and enrollment of the organization started seriously dwindling. Consequently, the staff was required to take a pay cut. Since the baby was an added financial responsibility, there was no way we could make ends meet. I also saw a serious reduction in staff members, particularly in the education department. This meant more job duties for those left behind. One advantage of being a house parent in a moment of financial strain is the fact that they have a pivotal role in how the organization runs. Without house parents, there would be no residential childcare. As a result, they are almost always the last ones to go.

I spent nearly twenty years at Bright Meadows Academy with virtually no regret. Although I was hired as a teacher, I spent a significant amount of time working in the house as a relief house parent. There were moments I became frustrated with other staff members and supervisors and other times I did not agree with how things were handled, but overall it was one of the best places to work. I gained valuable experience and taught just about every class imaginable, from science to music appreciation. Of course I had moments of failure, but they believed enough in me to give me another chance to learn from my mistakes. I cannot count the number of students I have interacted with, but why would I want to? Being in the center of God's will was a reward in and of itself. Did I form positive relationships with staff and students? Absolutely! Many people I've come to consider my friends at Bright Meadows I still keep in touch with. Did I gain valuable experience? Definitely! Before I was hired, I had no idea what it was like to live in a foreign country or how to effectively deal with troubled youth. Bright Meadows not only taught me these skills, but also how to be a better teacher and youth care worker overall. For that, I am eternally grateful!

PART 3:
THE WORST OF TIMES

As much as I loved working at Bright Meadows Academy, staying was not a viable option. Before I left, one of the department heads made a passing comment before I left: She said "Good luck finding another school like ours!" I didn't think much of the comment and dismissed it as a snide response to my leaving. Looking back now, however, I view it as almost a prophetic comment; did she really know something that I was overlooking? I knew Bright Meadows was a truly unique school, but how unique was it? After our interview, I had high hopes for Dark Hills Academy and actually looked forward to starting a new life and a new career. Unfortunately, what I thought was going to be a rewarding career ended up being a nightmare full of lies, humiliation, hypocrisy, and overwork. As horrible as my experience was, my goal in writing this section is not to mudsling; if that were its purpose, I would have used actual names and locations. My ultimate goal is to show some of the many negative trends within residential child care observed at Dark Hills as well as possible danger signs.

TANKS, PENDULUMS, AND "NICE NICE" PHILOSOPHIES

After moving in and getting our business taken care of, my wife and I started our observations in the cottage. While we were there, one of the students, Cameron, refused to eat his vegetables. Cameron was ten years old and very outspoken. When the house mother confronted him for not eating his vegetables, Cameron impudently told the house mother that he was not going to eat them. What started off as a minor confrontation turned into a standoff with neither side giving into the other one. Ultimately, the vegetables weren't eaten and the incident was never mentioned. Another incident that I clearly remember was when the house father I was training under was supervising the students in the gymnasium. One of the students, Aiden, who was mentioned earlier, walked out of the gym without permission because he didn't like the way a game was progressing. When the house father tried talking to him, Aiden continued to walk away.

My first thought to both of these incidents was "These students never would have gotten away with this at Bright Meadows." These incidents also worried me because it seemed like a foreshadowing of things to come. I vowed then and there that these incidents would never happen when I became the house father. Even though the structure was much looser than Bright Meadows, I felt like my child care experience would guide me through. Sadly, this was not the case; my wife and I dealt with so much disrespect and insubordination from the students that it was overwhelming at times. All of the psychology and de-escalation techniques did not seem to quell the overwhelming amount of disobedience that we dealt with on an almost daily basis. It didn't take me long to realize that this was no Bright Meadows.

True, perhaps we didn't handle every situation the best to our ability. At the same time, I saw that other house staff were having very similar issues with disrespect and acting out. Some organizations like Dark Hills have an overall negative school climate. In a regular school, boarding or otherwise, you have various groups of students, ranging from very negative behaviors and attitudes to very positive and motivated ones. If the school is truly a therapeutic school, the very negative behaviors will many times transition to those that are somewhat tolerable. They may think negative thoughts, but there is much less acting out. Some schools are what I consider holding tanks for students. In other words, students are sent to a school that will keep them until that student is old enough to be on his own. Since there is no therapy taking place on the campus itself, behavior does not change and the student is just as negative, if not more, than when he first arrived. Organizations that are mere holding tanks do nothing more than baby sit students for an indefinite amount of time.

Dark Hills Academy could definitely be classified as a holding tank. In addition to keeping students or clients indefinitely without any therapeutic intervention, there are also no constructive plans for the future made for the student. Although a number of kids would talk to a counselor who was off campus, there was no real therapy being done with the students through the organization itself. Administrators and directors were convinced that the daily schedule alone was enough to impact the students' lives. It is true that a structured day brings stability and security to a student's life; however, if an organization does very little to deal with the emotional and behavioral issues, the student will not change for the better. This is what makes the mission statement so important; if there's no purpose, there's no standard to go by. Just as pollution will ruin a small pond, excessive negativity and insubordination can ruin a small holding tank of a school. Even students who have the desire to try hard in school and do well at the house are easily dragged down by the negative school climate. No structured day in the world can alleviate this unless something else is done to give the students hope. Even positive reinforcements and incentives do not work unless there is a structure to support it. Whenever my wife and I rewarded positive behavior with snacks or trading cards, students would have a sense of expectation about getting rewarded instead of being thankful.

When a new student arrives at a residential school, they usually go through a period known as a honeymoon period. After their belongings are inventoried and checked for contraband, they say good-bye to their care givers and start learning about the program. They are usually very quiet during this time because many of them are stunned from the dramatic change in their lives and are busy trying to learn how to live in this strange environment. Within a month of placement, some of them will begin acting out and become more rebellious. If the other students are acting positively within the confines of the structure, the new student's behavior will normalize. With several of the new students who entered Dark Hills, however, the opposite thing happened. I can think of at least ten students off the top of my head who came to Dark Hills Academy initially with pleasant dispositions and good attitudes. As the weeks and months progressed, however, their attitudes disintegrated and they were no longer the helpful, positive influences they started out as. For lack of a better metaphor, the good apple was spoiled by the other bad apples.

How the administrators and supervisors respond to disciplinary issues can determine how effective the program runs. First of all, supervisors should always support the staff regardless of the situation. The shoplifting episode mentioned in the second part of the book was a perfect example of staff members being unjustly punished for the misbehavior of the student. If the staff member is the cause of the misbehavior, it should be used as a training issue instead of a point of derision and ridicule. Youth care workers who feel supported should be able to take constructive criticism and be willing to try things differently. Under no circumstances should the supervisor ever harshly correct or openly ridicule the staff member. If the powers that be do not show respect for the workers, the students will not respect the workers either. Staff members should never feel like failures if they feel the need to call the on call administrator. Mike, one of my supervisors at Dark Hills, resented me for calling him for disciplinary issues. When I watched him deal with misbehavior, all he did was holler at the students. I came to the sad conclusion that calling him was fruitless.

Moreover, since calling was a sign of weakness in his eyes, I stopped calling him altogether and dealt with the situation as I saw fit.

Secondly, the on call administrators need to have a system for dealing with discipline and what to do in cases of a behavioral emergency. Too many times at Dark Hills I had a student acting out and I was unable to contact the on call administrator. Even Bright Meadows had similar issues, but not as frequently. Luckily, none of the situations ever turned violent or even escalated beyond raised voices. Usually, the reason I wasn't able to get a hold of them was either due to bad cell phone signals or being off campus running an errand. If the administrator is ever off campus, the staff should always be notified and told who to reach in case of emergency. Crisis training can be a very valuable tool for staff members who work with volatile students on a daily basis.

Most importantly, administration should have a no tolerance and no nonsense policy toward discipline. What I admired about Bright Meadows was the fact that their punishment was austere, yet not abusive. It also effectively matched the severity of the infraction. Several students complained that the punishment was unfair and abusive, and one ex-student even wrote a book about how she was abused at Bright Meadows. It is my conviction that this ex-student would have complained about her treatment at any boarding school she was at. Larry, another supervisor at Dark Hills, had no particular methodology of giving discipline. Most of the time, disobedient students simply sat in his office for an indefinite period of time while Larry listened to opera and did his paperwork. Although being bored and listening to Bizet's <u>Carmen</u> may be considered cruel and unusual punishment by their standards, this does not really teach the student the error of his ways.

At the beginning of one of the school years, the administrators sat down with the boys of Dark Hills and explained that there would be a "no tolerance" policy for the up and coming school year. Moreover, any students that caused trouble would be expelled immediately and replaced by the countless number of students who wanted to be there but were on a waiting list. What sounded promising turned out to be nothing but empty threats. That particular school year, I saw many holes punched in walls and plate glass windows broken, various signs of physical and sexual abuse from other students, students running away, a few incidents of theft, and countless incidents of overt disrespect. Although many students were dismissed, several infractions occurred before this action took place. The long term students were allowed to remain for no particular reason.

If an organization is going to accept students who are high risk, they should be able to assess the risk objectively and determine accurately that this would be the right placement for him or her. Too many times at Dark Hills, we were not notified of any supervisory concerns. As mentioned earlier, these types of notifications are crucial for direct youth care workers so they know to watch for while they are on duty. Even knowing the student's general family background can be helpful. For example, if a student comes from a divorced family or has lived in abject poverty, the staff could be more sensitive to these issues and understand how to effectively deal with the students. Keep in mind I do not advocate invasion of privacy or breech of confidentiality in any way. All a staff member needs to know is basic information and what to be aware of.

If an organization is going to have a "no tolerance" policy, they need to seriously limit the number of chances a student is given. While we were still working at Dark Hills, there was a student named Richie. Richie was dismissed from Dark Hills due to disciplinary issues and then was re-enrolled a year later. He was fairly compliant for the first month or so, but his behavior took a serious turn for the worse. He punched holes in walls, intimidated other students, and struggled with anorexia. The whole time Richie was with us, Larry kept threatening to expel him but avoided doing so for one reason or another. The more the inevitable was procrastinated, the worse Richie's behavior became. As sad as Richie's personal life was, Dark Hills was not properly equipped to handle a student like this. There were several other students who were dismissed from Dark Hills due to disciplinary issues and then re-enrolled the same way Richie was. Sadly, the majority of them were expelled a second time due to similar disciplinary issues. Pathos and sympathy can create a real heart for service, but it goes too far when it clouds good judgment.

Even Bright Meadows found itself not putting parameters on out-of-control behavior. A year before I left, they accepted a sixth grader named Tara. Tara was not only too young for the program, her behavior was much too violent and unpredictable. Nevertheless the school director had a real heart for Tara and purposed in his heart to not give up on her. While she was at Bright Meadows, she did several hundreds of dollars of property damage and injured at least two staff members who were on duty. Even when she was taken to a lock-down facility due to a violent outburst, the school director welcomed her back, despite staff objections. Physical acting out is par for the course in just about all residential facilities; however, an organization should never tolerate perpetual acting out without either dismissing the student or at least making drastic changes to their disciplinary procedures.

An organization should also be well equipped to take on sensitive issues. For example, if a student suffers from sexual abuse, these issues should be dealt with by the organization as a whole and not just a psychologist who is off campus. Otherwise, it is a waste of time and money for the student to be at that particular organization. While my wife and I were at Dark Hills, the issues ranged from hoarding, to anorexia, to pornography, just to name a few. When the issues became too much to handle, the student was simply dismissed. In the course of a year, at least fifteen students were expelled from Dark Hills because they were unable to take care of the disciplinary issues. Some students were even told by the director that they would never succeed without Dark Hills' aide.

Most child care facilities go through a disciplinary cycle in their lifetime. An organization may have strict disciplinary procedures with all of the staff enforcing these procedures. However, within the course of about three years or so, new staff may come in and view the organization as too strict and unknowingly not support the discipline policies. Administration may also view the punishment as too strict and lighten up on the austerity of the discipline. As a result, students take advantage of the situation and try to get away with more misbehavior. The more this progresses, the more negatively the school climate will be affected. After a year or two of lackadaisical discipline, the administration may realize what is happening and start cracking down on acting out behavior. My supervisor Larry referred to this as a "disciplinary pendulum" that tends to swing from time to time. Long term students will frequently compare the present condition of the school to what it used to be like. Either they will say,"They don't let you do anything anymore" or "They let students get away with too much" Poorly run organizations do not have this pendulum swing; they either stay with being too strict or too lax.

A disturbing trend that I have observed over the past few years is the adoption of what I call the "nice nice" approaches to discipline. I believe there are staff members and organizations that tend to be abusive toward their clients. Some have even been rightfully shut down due to this issue. However, the staff members and administrators should be in control of the discipline at all times without being too abusive. Some modern approaches to discipline give some power and authority to the students in hopes of teaching self accountability. If utilized too much or used on the wrong group of students, this could lead to rebellion, and anarchy, in some cases. This exact thing happened to my supervisor Mike when he worked at a reputable boarding school. While he was there, the school adopted one of the "nice nice" philosophies to an otherwise well-functioning philosophy of discipline. Within a few months, a campus-wide riot broke out and the police had to be called in to quell the insurrection. Mike wrote a statement to the media, explaining what happened, blaming the outburst to the sudden change of discipline. The directors were apparently more outraged at Mike's statement to the media than at the riot itself.

This is not just one isolated incident. I have spoken to several different camp counselors and house parents who complained that students were given way too much freedom and not enough accountability. As a result, behavior became unmanageable, causing frustration and burnout of the staff. A possible reason for the increase of student-centered discipline and "nice nice" philosophies is the dread of being sued or slandered for physical or mental abuse. Another possible reason is that most organizations are functioning under the delusion that "nice nice" philosophies are somehow effective, when in actuality, they are not. Working with students who have behavioral management issues is one thing, but if there is no practical and effective disciplinary protocol, students will learn absolutely nothing and continue in their destructive ways

THE DEVIL'S WORKSHOP

During the interview process at Dark Hills Academy, I asked Joe, one of the interviewers, about the kinds of activities the students took part in. I knew that activities were not only valuable for young boys, but a necessity in childhood development. Joe told me all of the "wonderful" activities that the students participated in while they were there. 4-H, Boy Scouts, campouts, and horse husbandry were just some of the few activities. He also said that the students had a very rigid schedule from morning till evening, seven days a week. This was one of the attractions my wife and I had to coming to Dark Hills; there seemed to be a plethora of activities for the students to grow and learn from.

During my observation and training, I watched as the students start their day with chores and personal hygiene. Most, if not all, residential care facilities begin the day with some kind of cleaning, both in the sleeping quarters as well as the rest of the cottage. As structured as the morning seemed to be, the afternoon and evening was quite a bit different. After school, the students played basketball and then went inside for supper. Once supper was over, some of the students cleaned the kitchen while the others sat around and played video games. On the second day of training, the morning was the same routine as was the evening, which was expected. Once again, the students played basketball, ate supper, and played video games. When it was our turn to be observed, sure enough, the students played basketball, ate supper, and played video games.

For over a month of being on duty, the students didn't seem to do anything beyond playing basketball, eating supper, and playing basketball. There was no 4-H program and Scouts apparently had not yet begun. The director complained to Mike, my supervisor, that the students were not doing anything constructive and that activities should be teaching them something. Although I totally agreed with Ron, the director, neither he nor Mike gave the house parents any suggestions as to what we could be doing with the students that would be a learning experience. The other house parents were in the same quandary as my wife and I were because they were told the same thing, yet not given any suggestions. Once Scouts started, the students were active and actually seemed to be enjoying themselves. Basketball practice was also an activity that most of the students enjoyed, but once basketball season was over, the unproductive evening schedule ensued.

The students' boredom began to manifest itself negatively in the house. The most noticeable thing was the amount of aggression and disrespect I began to see. Several times I took the students to play dodgeball in the gym. What was intended to be a fun, friendly game turned into a gruesome demonstration of bullying and a sadistic desire to hurt others. The students wanted to play dodgeball almost on a daily basis, but too many students, especially the younger ones, were getting hurt. Students also began quarrelling among themselves more frequently and destroying their own property. Compliance with the house parents also became an issue. They openly complained about everything and did not want to participate in suggested activities. Even the quality of their morning jobs suffered.

The director saw what was happening and blamed the inadequately trained house parents instead of taking a small iota of responsibility. As a result of the overall negative behavior, the students were forbidden to play video games or watch television during the week. This only exacerbated the situation instead of making it better. Students still remained agitated and aggressive and openly resented not being able to play their video games. One morning, the students refused to do their chores properly and the house looked unkempt. In his annoyance, Mike demanded that the house be "shut down." ("Cottage" and "house" are terms used interchangeably; both refer to the students' domicile.) When I asked him what it meant, he said that the students would not be able to participate in their normal activities and had to clean instead. I understood that the students had to redo their cleaning, but I still had no idea what he meant by shutting the house, especially since the students were not allowed to do anything anyway.

The summer brought on a unique and more difficult problem. After the second week of May, the school would only be half time and students would be at the cottage for the remainder of the day. This meant that the house parents were solely responsible for all supervision of the students, which meant that we had to do everything in our power to keep them occupied. Outdoor activities were not a viable option because most days it was way past 90 degrees with a dangerous heat index. Luckily, the pool was open for at least two hours a day for the students to swim. The last summer we were there, however, the pool did not open till late June and students had to wait. The other advantage of the summer program was I had greater flexibility to take the students to places like the library or the park. Sadly, the school was located in an isolated town with very little to do, which seriously limited what we could do with the students.

Some weeks, school was shut down for days at a time, leaving my wife and me with the students from wake-up to bedtime. For the first day or two, the students were amused with going to the park or library, but easily tired of these places. With five solid days with being on duty with the students, my wife and I were rapidly starting to run out of ideas. We were also exhausted after every shift we did from working an obnoxiously long amount of time; most weeks during the summer, we would work anywhere from 60 to 80 hours a week with no break or change in pay. Our job seemed to turn from youth care workers to baby sitters whose sole purpose was to keep bored students entertained.

To Dark Hills' credit, the chaplain did plan activities with visiting youth groups, such as afternoon games, barbecues, and other teenager-friendly activities. One of the issues I had with this was the fact that the interactions were not longer. Supervision was also an issue. Many of the girls from the youth group did not know how to dress or act appropriately around boys. Any time something happened, like excessive flirting or rowdy behavior, house parents were automatically blamed for any misbehavior while the visiting staff members were never held accountable for their negligence. Sometimes students were not allowed to participate in fun activities with the youth group for no apparent reason.

What Dark Hills Academy needed was more staff members to aide in activity planning, especially during the summer months. After being evaluated by an outside source, it was determined that Dark Hills needed to hire at least four more staff members to run more effectively. It goes without saying that the fewer staff members an organization has, the more responsibilities the existing staff have. The more responsibilities staff members have, the more inevitable staff burnout will be. The majority of house parents have a propensity to create activities for their students, but they can only do so much in this area. It is sad that many Christian organizations are poorly understaffed, leaving the ones who are employed there way overworked. It's also interesting that the amount of unassigned supervision always fell upon one particular department. Even at Bright Meadows, the brunt of extra responsibilities seemed to fall on the shoulders of the education department. At Dark Hills, it was the house parents who had to pick up the slack.

At Bright Meadows Academy, we had staff members whose sole responsibility was to plan activities for the students. The staff on duty worked in conjunction with the activity planner to ensure the students had plenty of constructive, and sometimes fun, things for the students to do. Activities ranged from planting gardens to chopping wood. The boys especially liked chopping wood because it was a constructive way to get their aggression out. The students at Bright Meadows also did community service with such companies like Habitat for Humanity and the Humane Society. Not only was it a good way to get to know people within the community, it also taught the students how to work for others with a charitable spirit.

There were times when administration at Dark Hills wanted the students to do outside work to keep them busy. Even though this was a very practical idea, it was also a challenge at Dark Hills. My wife and I worked feverishly to teach the students how to have a proper work ethic. Unfortunately, the students were never really rewarded or paid for the work they did. Sometimes the administrators rewarded the students with candy or ice cream, but the rewards were inconsistent to mean that much to the students. Some of the older students actually negotiated with the managers to have part time jobs, like cleaning offices or maintaining the swimming pool. Younger students were not given these responsibilities because they were thought of as too young and irresponsible. It was not surprising that students frequently complained when they had to outside chores and did a very poor job.

One of the most important things an effective youth care facility should strive to teach their clients is a strong work ethic. Daily chores are important, but they are only a fraction of what a child care facility can do to teach personal responsibility and money management. Even in my personal upbringing, I remember having a job cutting grass and earning money from it. Although most states do not allow students below the age of 16 to handle motorized equipment, there is no reason why the younger students could not do jobs like raking mowed grass or cleaning the outside of a house and get paid for it. Earning money and working hard also gives the student a strong sense of accomplishment and makes them appreciate what they have even more.

Having a structured environment goes hand in hand with constructive activities. When school was only half time during the summer, there was no set schedule. The only exception to this rule was when youth group activities were planned for the students. Most of the students who come from troubled backgrounds have unstructured lives that are totally unmanageable. An organization should have a consistent structure all year round with plenty of constructive activities. Even though summer may be a less structured time for the majority of boarding schools, the structure should never be compromised. In fact, the summer is the perfect opportunity to do things students were otherwise unable to do, like tending a garden or working out in the community.

A program that lacks adequate structure sets everyone up for failure, both staff and students alike. There is also no reason why both teachers and house parents, as well as other staff on duty, cannot help plan and participate in activities around campus. I have found that the more staff interact with students, the more influence they will have in their lives. There is an old cliché that it takes a village to raise a child. This is definitely the case at any youth care facility. Staff should also be given flexibility to do different things around their community. At Dark Hills, there was so much paperwork and special permission that had to be obtained that it wasn't worth the effort to plan such activities. Although it is primarily the house parent's role to plan activities, there is such thing as requiring too much planning of one person. If a rigid schedule is not kept and structure is not maintained, it will cause frustration for everyone involved.

PRIVATE TIME AND FAMILY

At a residential child care facility, privacy is virtually non-existent. First of all, the living quarters are extremely close to where the students are. Even with the door closed, the gist of most conversations and telephone calls can be heard by students or anyone outside. Secondly, the students have an acute ability to read people on the emotional level. The majority of them come from broken families who are constantly fighting or in turmoil. Many of these children know that divorce or a breakup is inevitable even before the parents themselves know. Needless to say that when teachers or house parents have any kind of skirmish or disagreement, the students can tell immediately that something is wrong, even if the staff member doesn't say anything. Some staff members are careless in their confidentiality and will indiscreetly blab clandestine information to students. This is especially true for students who have poor boundaries.

Living on campus also limits the amount of necessary away time a staff member may need. An apartment in the same building where the students live is even worse. On days off, my wife and I could hear every staff confrontation and every raucous action of the student. This was especially bad when we were trying to sleep in. Since our bedroom was adjacent to the main area where the students congregated, the noise of vacuum cleaners, clanging dishes, and loud voices resonated throughout the house. It seemed like the only way our family could have any kind of peace was after the students went to school. The evenings weren't as bed, since we usually had the television running or were looking after our daughter. Our apartment did not have a separate door, so anytime we went shopping we had to walk through the student living area.

As I mentioned in a previous chapter, house parenting is not only a job, it is a way of life. Even with this in mind, staff members still need some personal time to themselves. Unfortunately, our first apartment really did not allow us to have personal time individually or as a family. In order to overcome this problem, my wife and I decided to take little overnight road trips to get away from the apartment for some peace and quiet. It was an excellent way to be away from the reminders of work as well as to see many parts of the country we had not seen before. Where we were living allowed us to see parts of Texas, Arkansas, Oklahoma, Louisiana, and Kansas, all states we had never visited before. It is interesting that an article I read on line after I left Dark Hills suggested one of the ways to avoid burnout was to take little trips with your family to get away from campus. The one advantage of working at a place like Dark Hills was the amount of vacation time we earned. Within the span of twelve months, we had at least five weeks of vacation time. Most organizations only have Thanksgiving or Christmas off; Bright Meadows required staff to work either Christmas or Thanksgiving to allow others to have time off.

Normally, time away allows staff to feel rejuvenated and ready to go back. However, no amount of time could make me feel better about working at Dark Hills. It seemed like every time we drove back on campus to go back on duty, a sense of dread and loathing came over me like a heavy, wet blanket. Granted, nobody likes for vacation time to end, but the thought of work should not have such a negative effect on a person. Toward the end of our stay at Dark Hills, things were so bad, my feelings of hopelessness and despair worsened. I mentioned to my wife on more than one occasion that I might be suffering from job-related depression. I surmised that my depression was not an emotional struggle, but a spiritual one. After months of prayer, I realized that Dark Hills had a very strong negative spirit associated with it and that working there was making my condition worse.

Is it normal to work in a ministry and feel depressed? I wouldn't necessarily say it was "normal", but I've seen it happen on several different occasions. Some believe that this happens because they are not depending on the power of God to help them through the hard times. While this may be true part of the time, it's not always the case. If an organization does not support its staff spiritually and professionally, burnout and depression is almost inevitable. My supervisor acknowledged my discontentment, but instead of talking to me about it, he dismissed it as the inability to deal with job stress. There are several books written about keeping the flame of ministry alive and dealing with trials and tribulations. However, so much of the writing deals with what the servant is doing wrong as opposed to perhaps what the ministry itself is doing wrong.

All through the New Testament, you read about all of the apostles, including Paul, enduring numerous hardships and persecution. Yet through all of it, they never ceased praising God. I thought frequently about this and brazenly compared my condition to the apostles'. Even though their hardships were infinitely harder, they thrived on the love, care, and encouragement of other Christians. At Dark Hills, there was very little, if any, spiritual support outside of our marriage and outside of family and friends who frequently prayed for us. The apostles were also passionate about their divine calling and did not question its integrity. Bright Meadows was full of people who supported each other and parents of students who prayed for the staff without ceasing. Dark Hills, on the other hand, was spiritually dead. The staff were few in number and did not support each other as they should have. The only other house parents who supported us also felt like there was a spiritual component missing from their positions.

My wife also had stresses of her own. At Bright Meadows Academy, this was never an issue because females were revered by staff and students alike. Any student who was caught disrespecting any females, especially the female staff members, were punished sternly. The reasoning behind this was that so many mothers from the broken homes of these students were put in positions of authority. As a result, the students acted out against their mothers and usually had low opinions of female authority. Bright Meadows tried to take women, particularly the house mothers, out of positions of direct authority and give them a more nurturing role. In return, the male staff members did all they could to stand up for the honor of the female staff. The house mother was regarded so highly, students weren't even allowed to sit in the same seat as the house mother. Although this seemed somewhat extreme, it did make a very distinct point about respect for the mother figures in the house.

At Dark Hills Academy, however, respect for females was not reinforced, or even taught. From the day my wife and I started working there, it always seemed like I had to defend the honor of my wife. The boys impudently argued, questioned, and walked away from my wife whenever she tried to hold them accountable to their actions. One student even had the effrontery to say that my wife's cooking was "crap". Other students were too familiar with my wife and had to be reminded that she was an authority figure and not their chum. Since administration did not see this as a serious enough issue, I had to be much more austere to protect my wife' dignity. Students also did their best to sow discord between my wife and me to get their way. This is very common in divorced families; if a child cannot get what he wants from one parent, he will try to get what he wants from the other parent. My wife and I had many arguments because she would say one thing and I would unknowingly do the opposite of what she said. Schools need to make the effort to teach the students, especially boys, that whatever their background is, females should be respected and not manipulated or slighted.

Having a child adds yet another complication to the role of house parents. At Bright Meadows, house parents were not allowed to get pregnant until after a full year of service. They recognized that pregnancy and children were a large responsibility and did not want the extra duties of parenthood to impede on the quality of their work. When we were hired at Dark Hills, we realized that taking care of our infant daughter would be difficult work in addition to being house parents, but we felt that our maturity and life experiences would compensate for that. We even decided to conceive another child while we were there under the false pretenses that we were handling family life and our work well. I heard of some house parents having as many as four children of various ages working at a child care facility. Looking back, there was so much added responsibility and stress associated with house parenting and regular parenting that I recommended earlier that couples not have children when they applied for a house parenting position.

The thing that makes having children such a chore as a house parent is the amount of protection I had to give to my daughter. Some of the students we worked with were potential bullies and sex offenders, and I shuddered to think what some of these students would have done to her or with her had she not been properly supervised. One set of house parents were rightfully upset when one of the older boys was teaching their toddling son how to bang his head on the table. The boys of the cottage were very intolerant of our daughter's behavior and would frequently scold her for getting in their way or making too much noise. Students also had a tendency to be jealous when the house mother paid too much attention to their child or gave their child more of something than the other students. Taking care of my child's needs and the students' needs eventually proved too much to handle. Although my wife helped out with our child's supervision, she too had her share of responsibilities.

With all of these stresses, it is no wonder that so many house staff leave their jobs defeated and unfulfilled. Although staff need to do what they can to keep up their spiritual life, this kind of ministry requires cooperation and support from all those involved. First of all, administrators need to respect staff members' time off. Even though my wife and I had about seven hours off in the late morning/ early afternoon, it seemed like Larry, our supervisor, was always calling us to take students to doctors' appointments, counseling sessions, off-campus school functions, just to name a few. If a student was ill and could not go to school, it was also our responsibility to watch that student for the entire day. I also had to chauffeur students back and forth from vocational classes. When my wife was the regular house mother, she had to take nearly two hours from some of her time off to go shopping and unload the groceries. Administration not only need to delegate some of the superfluous responsibilities to other staff members, they really need avoid calling staff members who are not on duty.

It is also important to watch out for your family's personal needs and wants as well your own. I know of at least three different couples in my career that left because of the desires of their spouses. The director of Bright Meadows used to have a saying: "If Mama ain't happy, ain't nobody happy." My wife and child were the biggest source of support and happiness in my life, and still are (my relationship with the Lord is supersedes all else, of course). My supervisor's wife lived across the country and only saw him a couple of times a year. I wasn't quite sure of their personal situation, whether they were divorced, separated, or whatever, but I thought it was peculiar that someone with a spouse would be so distant from the one they were allegedly married to. I could never imagine being separated from my wife for a whole week, let alone indefinitely. Although your calling is extremely important, taking care of those whom you are tied to is that much more important. Sacrificing a marriage for the sake of any kind of career or ministry is a total disregard for the sanctity of marriage.

A ministry-oriented career can be one of the most rewarding choices you can ever make. However, a Christian or any other youth care worker needs to know their limitations and know when their particular ministry is not going well. If feelings of hopelessness and depression are prevalent, I believe that the youth care worker really needs to examine their future at that particular organization and whether or not they should stay there. Keep in mind I do not advocate quitting on the spot or quitting over a few frustrations a person may have. All ministries and careers have hardships associated with them, whether they are personal or otherwise. Nevertheless, if a job is creating crippling stress on the individual worker or on a marriage, it is time to start looking for work elsewhere. In this troubling economy, it is not a good idea to resign a post without having a job in hand first. I firmly believe that God does not call Christians to be miserable in their callings; amid trials, stresses, and tribulations, those who are truly called to ministries that are sincere in the furtherance of the Gospel never lose the joy and compassion that they had when they first started. It is also important to remember that those who resign from a ministry are not failures. Everyone has their own particular needs and personal situation that influence his or her decision; as long as the motives are pure, God will honor any decisions made.

IN THE EYES OF GOD AND MAN

The title of "Christian" is one that should not be taken lightly. If an organization calls itself Christian, it should uphold Biblical values and should do all it can to instill the message of the Gospel to all those it touches. Too many people and places use the term "Christian" when they actually don't use it in the context it is meant. Other places believe that "Christian" means nothing more than having very basic Christian ideals with a Bible class and a few devotionals tacked on. I firmly believe there is a much greater accountability, spiritually and otherwise, to organizations that actually use the name of Christ.

Dark Hills Academy is one such organization that advertises itself as a Christian boarding school. At the same time, there were many different things that we observed that did not reflect Christianity. One of the things that I saw while I was there was the lack of Bible studies and discipleship. Like most, if not all, Christian schools, they used a Bible based curriculum and had devotion time every morning before school. The other house father and I also had devotion time with the students at the breakfast table. Basically, I read from the Scriptures and had a discussion about what we read. I found this time to be an encouraging start to the day, and the students seemed to really enjoy it. When the other house father talked to Ron, the director, he recommended that we not do devotions at the house because he didn't want the students to get too much Bible. I don't know what Bible he was using, but my Bible, according to Isaiah 55:11 says that God's Word will never return void. It doesn't say anywhere in Scripture that one can read the Bible too much. Other than going to church twice a week, the students had a Bible study every Monday evening. The one who led the Bible study was an elderly gentleman named George who taught a Bible lesson and prayed with the students. George was an elderly gentleman from the community who came to do Bible study with the students out of the goodness of his own heart. It seemed like I was always confronting the students during George's devotion time or in church for chatting, falling asleep, or clowning around. I realize that these behaviors are typical for young boys, but it seemed like the confrontations for these outbursts were limited to us house staff. Moreover, very few, if any, of the students expressed any desire to grow spiritually and seemed disrespectful during church time.

As a Christian, there was nothing sadder than a "Christian" school that had no interest in expanding their spiritual scope to include things other than a few devotions and church services. It was apparent that there was no emphasis on the students' spiritual lives because their actions reflected it. Out of the year and a half I was at Dark Hills, only one or two students made serious commitments to the Lord. Once the commitment was made, however, there was nobody there to guide that new believer in the right path. Consequently, there was no change in behavior and the students went back to their carnal mindset. The majority of the time administrators were not even at Bible studies, which set a bad example for the students.

Most Christian schools have chaplains to help keep the spirituality alive on campus. Dark Hills actually had two different chaplains during my stay as a house parent. The first one, Donald, happened to be the son-in-law of the director. He was a quiet man, but seemed somewhat standoffish to many of the students. He was very good at planning activities with visiting groups, but was seldom active in the student body. If a staff member is going to have a positive impact on the students' lives, they need to be readily available for all students and not just a select few. Todd, the second chaplain, was much more outgoing and interacted much more freely with the students. He too did a phenomenal job planning activities for visiting youth groups and was much easier to talk to. The major issue I had with Todd was his poor judgment in certain cases. I remember one time he bought a student a Black Sabbath CD for some odd reason. Although I have no real qualms about people's musical tastes, the student that received this CD had serious spiritual issues and listening to Black Sabbath only worsened his mood. Both chaplains were respectable, but in my view, did not do enough to promote the Gospel or make new disciples.

The chaplain at Bright Meadows was one of the most effective spiritual leaders I met bar none. He showed a genuine interest in the students and all of the students felt more than comfortable to confide in him. He really pushed the need for discipleship and spiritual accountability for staff and students alike. He was not presumptuous in any way, yet showed a genuine interest in the staff members' lives as well as the students' lives. It was obvious that he loved the Lord and always seemed to put others first. I could write for another whole page or two what the Bright Meadows chaplain did for our campus, but suffice to say that he really embellished on the Christian aspect of the school.

Even though an effective chaplain can be of great value to any Christian organization, it is the leadership that sets the spiritual mood. If the director shows no interest in spiritual things, there is nothing that the chaplain can do to make the school climate any godlier. Ron was more concerned with the Scouting program and public relations than he was about the furtherance of the Gospel. Whatever vision a leader may have for his organization, if God is not at the center of the everything that is said or done, the school is no different than any other secular organization. I worked at Dark Hills Academy for nearly a year and a half and I can say with all sincerity that except for the occasional Bible study and devotion, there was nothing distinctively Christian about it.

What was also confusing about Dark Hills was how they classified themselves. When my wife and I interviewed, Ron told us that the main reason why students came to their school was for academics. He claimed that the students who enrolled at Dark Hills were behind in school and it was Dark Hills' responsibility to help them catch up and reach their academic potential. What I found particularly interesting was that their mission statement was to make upstanding citizens. Not only was this mission statement extremely vague, it made no mention of academics. Ron also said that Dark Hills accomplished their mission statement through Scouting activities. Several of the churches viewed Dark Hills as a ministry that took in students who were rejected by their families and by society in general. With all of the confusion behind the philosophy and mission statement, it was a small wonder that my wife and I had no idea what the administration hoped to achieve in the lives of their students.

One of the most sacred and special of holidays on the Christian calendar, aside from Easter, is Christmas. As a Christian school, it is important to teach the true reason of the season; you need to teach them that it is not about gifts and presents, but about the birth of our Savior and ultimate gift He gave us. Dark Hills did a shameful job in this area. Since churches were under the delusion that our students were poor and destitute, their giving was to a point of excessive. Granted, there were some boys who lived in substandard housing or in abject poverty, but many of them came from middle class families. Some families exceeded the average income, yet what all of them received for Christmas was appalling in amount. The amount of toys, clothing, gift cards, and cash each student received totaled well over $700. Some churches gave over $4000 to Dark Hills in cash and gifts.

Although there is nothing wrong with accepting charity and contributions, there were a couple of things that were disturbing, aside from the sheer amount of money and gifts each student received. First of all, I believe that the money could have been put to a better use. Several appliances and other cottage fixtures were in disrepair; the money the churches spent on the students could have been used to replace or fix these things, making the cottage more functional and appealing. Secondly, the churches were misguided in their thinking, hoping that their generosity would benefit the general welfare of the allegedly impoverished children. Instead, all it did was intensify their avarice, selfishness, and sense of entitlement.

Thirdly, this kind of indulgent giving did not seem fair to children of staff members, who received significantly less. Even though I wouldn't have wanted my child to receive the excessive number of gifts, it would seem unjust if my child were older to see other children her age receiving so many more gifts. The majority of the toys were carelessly broken by students and gift cards were spent on either candy or more toys that the students did not need. If I were one of those congregation members that gave gifts like that, I would have felt like my money was misused and wasted. Joe, one of my supervisors at Dark Hills, admitted himself that the students were spoiled by all of the gifts and acted brattier around the holidays.

One of the more affluent churches even held a fund raiser for Dark Hills Academy. During the holiday season, they hired a well known Christian band who gave a performance to hundreds of attendees. In the middle of the concert, a slideshow was shown of Dark Hills and one of the bigwigs of the church adulated the ministry, calling it "a God thing." Once again, the church was deluded into thinking that Dark Hills was a ministry to help rejected boys. It is my belief that Ron wanted affluent churches to think this to encourage generous donations. Dark Hills even hired a person solely in charge of fund raising to promote Dark Hills as a "poor boy" ministry to rich churches in hopes of getting donations.

Public relations is something that can be of great benefit to any organization, Christian or otherwise. Schools, especially Christian or religious schools, that do not interact with their community on a regular basis are often viewed with suspicion and sometimes even seen as cultish. Some correctional schools prefer to keep a low profile in their community because they do not want to be feared or blamed for the type of clientele they have. If a school is doing an effective job with discipline management, the community should have nothing to worry about. Communities can also help in the area of fund raising and sponsorship. Some businesses may not only donate funds to a school, but may also provide goods and services to schools that they have a good working relationship with.

In light of all of this, a school needs to be honest and upfront concerning their mission statement and their practices. What bothered me about Dark Hills was that no one in the community really understood what kind of school they were. Even my wife and I didn't understand the true purpose of the school. One day the emphasis could be on academics and other days it was about helping boys in need. Keep in mind I do not object to changing philosophies and mission statements. I believe that God can call ministries to serve other functions. For example, Bright Meadows was going to start out as a school to train teenagers to be missionaries. As time progressed, however, it was decided by its founder that they would be a Christian correctional school. A decision like this took quite a bit of discussion and prayer from not only the founder, but the board members as well. It was not a decision that was made quickly or taken lightly.

Furthermore, if a school is going to endorse organizations like 4-H or Boy Scouts of America, they must do it with the utmost of integrity. Another deception that Ron took part in was how he ran the Boy Scouts. Within the Scout program, there are several things that fellow Scout members have to vote on. Two of which are The Order of the Arrow and the rank of Eagle Scout. In order to get these titles, a certain percentage of students have to vote "yes". A fellow Scout member votes positively if he believes the candidate upholds all the positive characteristics of a true Boy Scout. Ron openly told the Scout members that they were required to vote "yes", throwing off the percentage. It apparently did not matter whether anyone thought the candidate upheld anything or not. It also seemed strange to me that so many of the Cub Scouts and Eagle Scouts did not uphold the list of positive characteristics of a Scout laid out in the Scout handbook. I personally doubt that the Boy Scouts of America would approve of this handling of their program.

Staff members also need to be truthful, honest role models for their students as well as to members in their community. Rick was a staff member at Bright Meadows who started in out in our wilderness program and transferred as a teacher to our American school at the start of the school year. As his supervisor, he was argumentative, incorrigible, and insisted on doing things his own way instead of how it was laid out in the manual. He was also grouchy with the students and had no qualms shouting at staff or students who made him angry. What made matters worse was the fact that he had an internet addiction (what kind of addiction is not important) and used the office computer to feed that addiction. Right there, Rick should have been fired from his post, but he was given an excessive amount of warnings to change his behavior. Sadly, his behavior never changed and was dismissed a year or so after his internet addiction was discovered.

It would be encouraging to hear that this was one of the very rare cases where role modeling was an issue. Unfortunately, other people at Bright Meadows were involved in such ignominious activities like gambling, prostitution, and petty theft. There were also a few staff that were arrested and charged with molestation of their students. Even though I am not Catholic, it is tragic that the Catholic church is held in such disdain by many people for the carnal sins of a few priests. Litigations are everywhere in our society today and as ministers of the Gospel, we need to be on guard. Most importantly, students are watching our every move and know much more than we give them credit for.

Staff members who commit these infractions do not realize the amount of damage control administrators must do in order to save the integrity of the ministry itself. The media seem to thrive on scandals, especially ones that involve Christian ministries. The more shocking the scandal, the more interested people seem to be. Even if a statement is made concerning the awareness of the crime, the reputation never fully recovers. Crimes against students can be even more devastating. If the infraction involves students, the ministry must deal with the parents and family members who are justifiably indignant about what has happened. Word of mouth can spread quickly about what happened and recommendations not to send a child there can have serious repercussions on enrollment. Administrators even have to deal with staff members who are affected by the public sin. Those who are guilty of public disgrace do not seem to be concerned with the ministry as a whole because they are too absorbed in their own pleasures and self-indulgence. Workers who are sensitive to the ministry as a whole and to the clients they work with realize the impact negative behaviors can have.

Just as God blesses nations that honor Him and casts judgment on those who condemn Him, God also blesses churches ad ministries that lift up His name in all they say and do. That is not to say that struggling Christian organizations are going through hardships because they are not honoring God. It's difficult to understand why corrupt ministries seem to prosper while ministries like Bright Meadows are struggling financially. What I do know is that all organizations that use the name "God" or "Christian" have a greater responsibility to their Creator and community than a secular organization. Otherwise, there is no need to use religious labels at all. Leaders and workers of any ministry have a special accountability that the secular world of business may not understand.

AUTHORITY AND *NOBLESSE OBLIGE*

Just about any organization needs some kind of director or CEO to keep the vision and the mission statement of the ministry alive. In the majority of non-residential Christian schools, it is the principal who is responsible for the maintenance of the school climate. However, in a residential school setting, it is the program director who ultimately supervises the youth care workers and department heads. They may have different names, but the program director is pretty much the same regardless of the organization. If an organization has a poor program director, chances are the school climate will suffer as a result. The question is this: What makes a good program director and how can you tell a good director from a bad one? This section could apply to just about any business and ministry.

First of all, a program director has to have love and appreciation for his staff as well as the students. Not too long ago when I started writing, I was watching a movie and heard the term *noblesse oblige*. I heard the term before, but was unsure of its meaning. According to the dictionary, it is the kindness authority figures are obligated to show subordinates. Working with children and teenagers can be tiring and demanding work, regardless of what talents you may possess as a teacher or house parent. A director should realize the task of being a youth care worker can be frustrating and arduous and at least express gratitude for the job being done. Although many program directors started out working with students, once they reach their position of authority, many of them stayed locked up in their offices, coming out once every so often, usually for public appearances or VIP visitors. It seemed like whenever Ron poked his head out of his office and there were no visitors, it was usually to express his discontentment or disapproval for what might have been happening at the time.

When I became a department head at Bright Meadows, I once asked my program director what I should focus on as a supervisor. He answered me in one terse sentence: "Keep your staff happy." It seemed like too easy of a solution, but sometimes the shortest answers are the best answers. The longer I worked for residential organizations, the more I learned that happy staff are productive staff. Keeping your subordinates happy does not mean giving them anything they want; it means to see to their needs, professional and otherwise, and addressing any problems and complaints they may have. When a supervisor does not appear to care about what the staff think, he can do serious damage to the staff's morale. If workers can be a part of the decision making processes, they may take more ownership of their job and actually feel a part of the program as a whole. The unhappiest of times at either Dark Hills Academy or Bright Meadows Academy was when I felt like I wasn't listened to.

Discretion and tact are also important for a program director. Staff members are going to make mistakes, no matter how efficient they may be. If confrontations need to take place, the supervisor needs to do it in the proper place at the proper time. One Sunday afternoon when my wife and I were on duty, Mike pulled me into the office and scolded me harshly for something I allegedly did. Not only did he overreact to a point of belittling me, he also did it at an improper time. It was extraordinarily difficult to go back on duty after being belittled. Ron was by far the worst for humiliating staff members indiscreetly. One time I borrowed the wrong staff van and he had no reservations of openly and tactlessly confronting me in front of the students. He even confronted supervisors as if they were misbehaving children.

Supervisors should also make an effort to socialize with their staff members. Having a good social relationship with the supervisor somehow makes the work so much easier. The CEO of Bright Meadows was a very social person and openly talked to staff and students about nearly anything. Whether it was a work related question or about how the family was doing, he always had time to talk to both the staff and the students. I did not always agree with the CEO's ideas, and sometimes he could be downright pushy, but I respected him because he showed me respect. Before I left, he gave me a great big hug and wished me all the best. He even offered me my job back should I ever want it. Any time I tried to strike up a conversation with Ron, the director of Dark Hills, he either seemed disinterested in what I had to say or responded as if what I said showed no insight whatsoever. Joe, on the other hand, was one of my supervisors at Dark Hills. He respected my ideas and input and was a frequent encouragement to me and my wife. Of all the supervisors at Dark Hills, it goes without saying that Joe was the only one I truly respected and trusted.

Open and honest communication is yet another important aspect of effective supervision. So many times I have heard staff members all over complain that they are kept out of the loop of what is happening. It's even worse when staff members are confronted for doing something or not doing something that their subordinates expected them to do, yet didn't tell them about it. A perfect example of this was when I was confronted for not sitting behind the students at church. Although I sat in the midst of the students and pled ignorance to the expectation, I was labeled a poor staff member for not keeping track of my students. Dark Hills was notorious for turning issues of ignorance and poor training into disciplinary issues.

I also felt like Ron was not honest during our interview process. During our visit, he told us about the ambitious building projects he was starting. According to his plans, he was building a new chapel, a new gymnasium, and several new cottages for the students. He even posted these plans on the Dark Hills website and bragged about how all of this was going to be built in the very near future. He also told my wife and me with our experience, we would be like the senior house parents, mentoring other new house staff in the new cottages. Basically, it sounded like a golden opportunity; it seemed like an expanding project that my wife and I would have been foolish to turn down. The reality was that Dark Hills fell on financially hard times and that there were no immediate plans to build any of these buildings. In fact, Mike told me that Ron had been saying the same thing to everyone for several years. It was at that point that I realized my wife and I made a huge mistake signing on as house parents at Dark Hills.

Needless to say this kind of treatment had a very negative impact on the staff morale. Steve, a fellow house father, was a very devout Christian man with a very even temperament. Ron frequently chided and belittled him, even threatening his employment. One time he even threatened to terminate him and his wife when his wife could not go back on duty due to being violently ill with the stomach flu. This mild-mannered and humble worker once told me that he had an urge to spit in Ron's face for the way he was treated. Toward the end of our stay at Dark Hills, I avoided talking to Ron at all costs for fear of being confronted for something trivial.

There was one set of house staff who came a couple of months before my wife and I did. They were hard working and loved doing exciting things with the students in their cottage. Daryl, the house father, was an ex-marine with a strong sense of discipline and Julia, his wife, was full of new ideas. They had a sincere desire to impact the lives of the students for the cause of Christ. It seemed like Daryl and Julia were always working on campus, even on their time off. When they weren't working with the Scouting program, they were interacting with the students in some way, shape, and form. Although they weren't anywhere near perfect, they were an asset to Dark Hills. The tragedy was they left after working there only four months. Why did they leave? The answer was simple: they did not get along with Ron.

It was unbelievable how many sets of house parents came and went at Dark Hills. My wife and I calculated that within a two-year period, Dark Hills Academy had ten sets of house parents for two houses (this includes a set of relief house parents). Even though residential schools usually experience a high turnover rate, this was excessive, even by this kind of school's standards. Nearly every set of house parents who left either left because of Ron's mistreatment or were terminated by Ron. Even the turnover rate for teachers was enormous at Dark Hills. Although one of them left due to a maternity leave, many of them were either laid off or left to find better jobs. What was really sad was that the average student stay was significantly longer than the stay of the teachers or house staff. For any organization, this kind of turnover can only mean one thing: not enough was being done to see to the needs of the staff.

Supervisors like the ones at Dark Hills seem to care more about the organization itself than they do about their staff. Yet they fail to realize that without high quality staff, their program would cease to exist. People like Ron ran their program with supreme authority and inflexibility. In the staff handbook, I read that the program director could fire any of the staff for any reason at any time. In a public school, this wouldn't happen without union involvement. However, poorly run Christian organizations somehow think they can have their way with the staff. An ex-supervisor at the first Christian school I taught at was terminated from his job without ever knowing why. When he asked, the school board refused to tell him. Not only is this kind of behavior unethical, it is totally inappropriate, whether it's a Christian or secular school.

With all of this said, it is too bad that some Christian schools do not have unions. One would think if the Holy Spirit controlled the hearts and minds of the administration, unions would be totally unnecessary. Sadly, too many Christian youth care workers feel overworked and underappreciated. Although there are those that can never be made happy, Christian leaders need to see to the overall well being of all their staff. They need to talk to their staff about their personal and professional needs. Even if nothing can be done to change policy and procedures, it is the director's responsibility to at least express a genuine interest in the staff's input and general well being. Most importantly, the program director of a Christian facility needs to understand that it is God's ministry and not his own; he is God's instrument to minister to hurting souls and hard working staff.

Directors should also foster a sense of community with their staff and students. Although they may not be able to afford high salaries and financial incentives, they should at least do kind things for them like take staff members out for a pleasant supper or plan school wide functions like picnics. Bright Meadows even awarded "Staff Member of the Month" to acknowledge a job well done. Larry did this once or twice, but was not faithful in doing it on a consistent basis. It may only be a sheet of paper, but it makes the staff member feel that what they do has value. School wide functions also allow the students to see the staff members in a non-disciplinary role, provided that everyone shares in the supervision. Most importantly, directors need to participate in these activities and help out when they can. Directors need to realize that they are only human as their staff members are. *Noblesse oblige* may be an uncommon word, but it should be common in Christian authority figures.

PART 4:
TERMINATION AND
CONCLUDING THOUGHTS

LIGHTNING STRIKES TWICE

My wife and I chose to be house parents at Dark Hills Academy in the hopes of being mentoring house parents to new couples coming in. Little did we know that not only was this not going to happen, but that we were going to face the hardest times of our lives. As I look back now, I see that so much handwriting was on the wall, but at the time we believed that things were going to work out for the best. Ultimately, things did work out for the best, but not without an abundance of humiliation, fear, and anger, feelings that should not be present in any of God's ministries. The dread and horror of termination is a time that no one ever wants to go through. Unfortunately, my wife and I had the displeasure of going through this terrible time twice.

The first of these horror stories started in July of 2009. My wife and I had been the regular house parents since April of that same year. Steve and his wife were the house parents before us, but were demoted to relief house parents after Steve was blamed for being responsible for one of his students shoplifting. When my wife and I were promoted to regular house parents, my wife had a bad feeling about it, but I was elated because I believed it was a sign of better things to come. Once we started working in the house, however, it didn't seem like we were doing anything right. Mike, my supervisor, was constantly telling me how I was letting the students control me and how messy the cottage looked. My wife was also told on a regular basis how much she antagonized the students, even though they were clearly the ones that were antagonizing her. Mike told me at the beginning of the month that he knew that my wife and I were not happy and even invited us to start looking for a job elsewhere, if we wanted to.

Mike's wife, Susan, pulled my wife and me aside a week later and told us that one of the reasons we were struggling as house parents was because of our insufficient training. She and her husband were going to remedy this by working with us. This meant that my wife and I would be observing Mike and Susan being the regular house parents for a week followed by them observing us as house parents for a week and giving us their input. It sounded like a good idea, since our training consisted of nothing more than doing the basic paperwork and watching the students play basketball and watch television. I was a little nervous about being observed because Mike and Susan were very critical people. Nevertheless, my wife and I both thought it would be a good idea to get the training we needed.

Then it happened. At the end of our shift on the third weekend of July, Mike and Susan pulled my wife and me into the office and told us that we were going to be replaced as soon as they could find a couple that would agree to start working. In the meantime, Steve and his wife were going to take our place as the regular house parents and we were going to be demoted as relief house parents. We asked about the supposed training that my wife and I were supposed to be receiving, but the issue was ignored altogether. They also told us that all of our belongings, which was a two-bedroom apartment full of furniture and personal belongings, had to be moved within two days. At that time, our big concern was what would happen to us once they found a couple to replace us. Would we be unceremoniously thrown out on the street with our stuff? Mike and Susan showed very little sympathy and told us that there was nothing they could do.

Needless to say my wife and I were crushed after this meeting. For the first time in our lives we faced the horrifying prospect of being homeless. At this point, it did not seem like we were given enough time to even get a job, let alone look for one. My wife cried bitter tears as she frantically tried to pack dishes and personal things into boxes. We tried to brainstorm some things we could do if worse came to worse, like move into the hotel that my wife's friend managed or store our stuff at my father-in-law's house, since our house was being rented. Feelings of shock and panic raced through our souls as we grappled with the idea of having to leave immediately. Joe, with the help of some students, helped us move our belongings, but it was carelessly done and several items were damaged as a result. People we called offered their prayers and support, but nothing seemed to take away the fear of destitution. We prayed more earnestly than we ever did before that God would deliver us.

A couple of days later, Ron came to the door to talk to us. He apparently saw some comments I had made on Facebook about how terrible of a place Dark Hills Academy was. Certain people warned me about posting negative things on the internet, but when I did it, I honestly could have cared less. His complaint was that we were making his program look bad and he saw it as nothing but cheap gossip. I then rebutted that I was very angry with him for throwing my wife and me out on the street. He was taken back by this comment and said that he never threw anyone out on the street in his life. He also told me that he never condoned Mike's decision to move our stuff so quickly and he invited us that if ever we had a problem to talk to him directly. At that point, it felt like things were not as bleak, but we still decided to look for another job.

Once Mike and Susan left, Larry became our new supervisor. He seemed like an objective fellow who was much easier to talk to. Since our job searches yielded nothing and things were running more smoothly under Larry's supervision, my wife and I decided to stick it out at Dark Hills for the time being. In early November, Larry gave all of the house staff their yearly evaluations. He admitted that they weren't as accurate as he would have liked them to have been and that they were only based on what he saw over the span of two months. Nevertheless, my wife and I got an average review with some minor points to improve upon. This was even worse than a poor review because not only did it not give us the input we needed to be better house staff, but it also gave us a false sense of security.

Over the course of seven months my wife and I worked as relief house staff with no complaints or areas of concern that needed to be addressed. There was an incident of me shouting at a student, but Larry simply told me not to raise my voice like that. I acquiesced and went on with business as usual. We were supposed to get another evaluation in March, but Larry consistently procrastinated, telling us he would give us one when he got the time. Since nothing was said about our performance whatsoever, my wife and I worked without any thoughts of termination. Larry was much more consistent and timely in dealing with disciplinary issues and did not appear to blame staff members for student misbehavior.

One morning in June Larry told my wife and me to meet him in his office so he could do our evaluation. Since our evaluation was nearly three months late, we thought it would be nothing more than a formality with no particular concerns. As we were given our evaluation, we were stunned to hear that Larry did not think my wife and I were a good match for Dark Hills and was giving us until the end of the year to find another job. The reasons he gave us for our termination were a complete surprise because all of the information he told us we had never heard before. According to Larry, some of the reasons for our termination included the poor supervision of our daughter, countless student complaints, and my attitude toward the position in general. He assured us he would wait till we found another job and that we would have medical coverage through Dark Hills until the baby was born (my wife was six months pregnant at the time). He also told us that he was aware that similar issues existed back when Mike and Susan were our supervisors.

Even though the situation did not seem as desperate as the first time, there were several issues that we had with our poor evaluation and pending termination. First of all, why were these issues not addressed before, especially since they had been hanging over our heads for nearly a year? There was no hint of a paper trail, no verbal or written warnings, and no improvement plans. True, we were talked to by Mike and Susan, but there were no specific things that they thought we should work on. We cannot improve on something we know nothing about.

The training we were supposed to have never came to fruition. Secondly, the evaluation was very badly timed. If our evaluation had taken place in March, when it should have been, it would have given me more opportunities to find a good teaching job. By the end of June, most schools have already hired their teachers for the year. Since there was no time to find a quality teaching job, I was forced to take a job as a telemarketer selling substandard life insurance, a job I regret taking. During this time, there was a student who was sexually assaulted by another student while my wife and I were sleeping. Even though Larry did not hold us to blame for what happened, it seemed like a very strong coincidence that we would get evaluated a little more than a week after the incident occurred. Thirdly, it seemed like the first evaluation he gave in November was nothing more than a lie. What's the point of having something on file when it is totally fabricated?

As the weeks progressed, Larry's attitude toward us seemed to take a turn for the worst. Larry not only changed the hours we were on duty, he also began requiring my wife and me to spend more time sleeping in the house. We went from working forty hours a week with two overnight duties to working fifty-six hours a week with four overnight duties. When I went to interview for the life insurance job, Larry had apparently interviewed a couple for the relief house parent position. If I had not been hired for the job, why would Larry interview couples if we were given until December to find another job? Either he told them that they were going to be hired as soon as we got another job, or his intent was to break his word and let us off early. When I told Larry that my wife and I would need more time to pack our stuff, he refused to give it to us initially, claiming that the new couple would need time to move their belongings in. I told him that if this were the case, my wife would not be able to be on duty with me so she could pack. He eventually gave into our request, but made us work more days to compensate for the time off. Steve and his wife, another set of house parents, faced the same unfair treatment during their moving process. The final injustice was when Larry told us that they would not let us have medical coverage, even though he had said earlier that we would.

THE DREADED TASK

Whether you are a youth care worker or an authority figure, nobody relishes the prospect of firing or being fired. Aside from feeling like a total failure, there is the fear of having your work record scarred by the negative experience. There are also feelings of anger, betrayal, or humiliation, depending on the circumstances. Some may even have a feeling of relief; it's as though their termination is permission to leave a job they otherwise dislike but are afraid to leave. From a supervisor's perspective, making the decision to terminate someone's employment is not easy either, especially if you have a good working relationship with the employee. You have the fear that if you fire the person, they will take it personally and hold the decision against you. Although nothing can make the process of termination easy, there are several things to remember.

First of all, it's important that the supervisor has clear and consistent communication with all of his subordinates. When I was a department head at Bright Meadows, I had a staff member who had worked there quite a bit longer than I did. He had a terrible attitude and his interaction with students was very poor. When I gave him his yearly evaluation, I gave him a very poor review. Needless to say he was indignant about the whole ordeal and complained to one of the other department heads. The other department head understood why the substandard teacher got a poor review, but he told me that the most important thing to do for a poor performance was to leave a paper trail. In other words, talk about specific issues before an evaluation so it is not totally unexpected. Once these issues are brought to the employee's attention, document it and keep copies. The staff member may disagree with the confrontation, but at least they are made aware of the issues at hand. Larry failed to mention any of the issues to my wife and me prior to the evaluation, so when we were given the reasons for our termination, it was a total shock to us.

As a youth care worker, there are some things that are serious concerns for supervisors, aside from illegal or immoral issues. Obviously, any actions that are in violation of what is in the manual are grounds for disciplinary action. Another thing that supervisors look for is a well structured environment, whether it is at the house or in the classroom. If administration is frequently called for disciplinary issues, it does not look good for the teacher or house parent, even if it is not their fault. If a staff member is overly authoritarian or permissive, the supervisor may also have something to say about this as well. It is even worse when a staff member gets physically aggressive with students; for liability purposes, that staff member may be taken out of the house or classroom right away.

Poor child care skills can lead to other problems if not dealt with in a timely fashion. There was a staff member at Bright Meadows that was way too passive with the students in his care. "Aw, c'mon guys" was the extent of his discipline. Even though he was in a house that did not require strict discipline, he did virtually nothing to ensure the students were doing what they were supposed to be doing. When he was on duty one night, the other students ganged up on one of the boys and pummeled his face. As a parent of the beaten up student, I would have demanded that staff member's resignation, if not some kind of reprimand. Lack of discipline on the administration's and staff member's part can be just as bad as too much discipline.

Normally if a teacher or house parent is doing something consistently wrong, it is the supervisor's responsibility to tactfully and directly inform that staff member of their errors. However, some supervisors may do a substandard job. The worker may go weeks or months without knowing there is ever a problem only to find out that they may face termination without warning. If this is the case, there may be some warning signs that may serve to help the staff member know if their job is in jeopardy. One of the first warning signs is how staff members, former or otherwise, had been dealt with in the past. When my wife and I started at Dark Hills Academy, we heard nothing but bad things about Jed and Lisa, the former staff members who were terminated shortly before we were hired. At first they sounded like terrible youth care workers, but the longer we were there, the more inconsistent the story was behind their actual departure. I also realized that the other sets of house parents were being equally mistreated and harshly disciplined. If they did not treat the other staff members with dignity, confidentiality, and respect, it seemed obvious that we would be treated the same way.

Another sign that a youth care worker's job is in danger is what may be written in the manual. In the Dark Hills Academy manual, it states that the director has the right to terminate his employees for any reason at any time. Normally, there is a protocol to follow for staff discipline. If a director has carte blanche to do what he wants with his staff's employment, this is nothing short of despotic rule. Joe, one of the administrators who was in charge of the Scout program, was unceremoniously demoted to helping with Scouts instead of running it. It was apparently an arbitrary decision made by Ron because Ron thought that someone else would be better for the post.

It also makes a difference of how much control the students have of the program itself. Aiden, who was well respected by Ron, the director, frequently visited the administrative office and talked to Ron for hours on end. It was interesting that staff members who did not get along with Aiden mysteriously resigned or found themselves without work. Aiden unabashedly told me of several staff members who were fired. When my wife and I had our doomed evaluation, Larry mentioned that certain students were complaining about our performance. As Larry was talking to us, I could not help but wonder who it was that complained and how much impact their complaints had. Although I do not discredit student input, any complaints should have been specific and dealt with in a timely fashion.

Staff members should never be fearful or suspicious of whether or not they face termination. If a job is not going well or if frequent mistakes are made, the staff member should be aware of the inevitable danger of losing their job. When I worked at the insurance company for only a month, I was aware that the job was not going well because I was not able to meet my quota. If an organization does not communicate with the staff member or does not leave a proper paper trail, there is no way to know what to improve on or that termination is inevitable. This kind of unacceptable behavior is nothing short of malice, indifference, or sloth.

Unlike being fired from a regular job, being laid off or fired from a house parent job or a job that requires you to live on campus poses a serious problem: where do you go when you lose your job? Obviously, the staff member needs to leave campus as they are done with their employment. If they have no job or if they have to leave as soon as possible, they run the risk of having nowhere to go. This is the issue my wife and I faced both times termination loomed over our heads. When I talked to Joe after he lost his position as Scout Master, he told me that it is always a good idea to have a "Plan B". If a position does not feel like it is working out, the staff member should not only start looking for another job, but also looking for an alternate place to go should unemployment become a reality.

Steve, the other house father, and I frequently talked about the many shortcomings of Dark Hills and even considered writing a list of grievances to the board members, since registering a list of formal complaints to the administration would be futile. Right before Steve left, I actually wrote up a list of grievances to submit to the board members. It was six pages long and I was only about half done with the list. As tempting as it was, I decided not to submit my list. First of all, I knew that the board members would blow it off as quickly as the administration would have. Ron and Larry were well respected, if not revered, by all of the churches and VIPs associated with Dark Hills Academy. I, on the other hand, would be nothing more than a disgruntled ex-staff member who was incapable of doing his job. Even if Steve and his wife signed their names to it, it would not have made it any more valid in the board members' eyes. Secondly, if Ron was crooked and dishonest in his dealings with me as a staff member, I could only imagine that if I made him angry, nothing would stop him in getting his revenge. Most importantly, Steve challenged me and my motives for composing the list of grievances. Was I doing it because I was concerned about other people, or was I angry and wanted to get revenge on those who made my wife and me miserable?

Before you leave, most places will conduct an exit interview. During the exit interview, the human resource person or administrator will ask questions in regard to your experience at the organization as well as things that the organization could improve upon. If the facility has any kind of integrity, even if they have no intention of changing certain policies, they should at least consider what the ex-staff member has to say. Unfortunately, places like Dark Hills Academy do not seem to care what ex-staff members have to say. Consequently, it is not surprising that organizations like these have such an alarming turnover rate. Schools and facilities ought to take into consideration why staff have the desire to leave and use this information to improve their overall performance. It would also potentially reduce the turnover rate if such improvements were made. Moreover, keeping staff longer would save the headache of looking for employees to replace the ones leaving. If workers stay around for longer, the amount of experience would increase dramatically and therefore improve the professionalism of the organization overall.

For weeks after my wife and I left, I couldn't help but wonder if the house parents that were still working there when we left were struggling as miserably as we were. It's not that I wanted them to suffer at all, but I wanted them to be aware of the injustices Dark Hills gave to ex-staff members like us. The fact of the matter is there are those who would feel content, and even thankful about working at this organization. Instead of wallowing in spite and self-pity, I figured that life would go on at Dark Hills Academy and wishing misery was wrong no matter what my reasons were. Once you leave an organization, life goes on. Unlike Bright Meadows Academy, there was no longer any need to stay in touch, since there were no real relationships built.

LESSONS LEARNED

As I look back at my nearly twenty years of experience as a teacher and youth care worker, there are several things that I have learned. First of all, there is a huge difference between teachers and house parents. When I was hired at Dark Hills Academy, I was under the false impression that the two positions were the same, much to my chagrin. There is also a big difference between being a teacher at a regular school and a teacher at a correctional school. As a teacher, although I have a great concern about the overall personal well being of each student, my concern is also for how well the students understand the material I am covering. With house parenting and teaching at a correctional school, there is way too much emphasis placed on supervision. When I am teaching a biology class, I am more concerned about the students understanding things like photosynthesis and mitosis than I am about what Jack and Jill are doing underneath the tables with their hands.

The second valuable lesson I learned was that Christian values are not always practiced at Christian schools. An organization might call itself "Christian," but there is no guaranteeing that how they deal with the staff or students is. It is sad that directors or supervisors act maliciously or dishonestly, yet still claim they are led by the Holy

Spirit. It is especially sad when organizations that claim to be Christian try to capitalize on the generosity and benevolence of churches in their affiliation. Christian schools also do not guarantee a tighter structure than a secular school. In fact, the students at correctional schools, Christian or otherwise, have a tendency to act out more than students who attend regular schools.

I also learned that working with my spouse was not as easy as I thought it was going to be. When my wife and I started out as house parents, I thought that having the most important person in my life working beside me and acting as my support would be the ideal situation. However, I learned that this was far from the ideal. There is nothing worse than disagreeing with your spouse when you are on duty, especially when it involves a student or a tricky situation. Many times I had to pull my wife aside to work out our differences while we were on duty. Several married couples have remarked that having children puts a strain on the relationship. It's especially stressful when you have eight children in the mix that aren't even yours. Thankfully, my wife and I worked out our differences in a timely fashion, so the job couldn't tear our marriage apart.

Yet another lesson I learned was that problems with poor leadership do not magically disappear. When Ron, the director, came to me saying that he never threw anyone out in his life and that I could talk to him any time there was a problem, I assumed that all was well, especially when Mike left and Larry came on as the new supervisor. We were further lulled into a state of complacency and security when my wife and I received the bogus evaluation in November. In retrospect, I should not have stopped looking for a teaching job, especially when I started feeling depressed. I learned too late that Mike, my old supervisor, was nothing more than Ron's puppet and that it was Ron's idea all along to put my wife and me out.

Before our termination meeting, I told Ron that if his school was planning on expanding, I would be interested in being a teacher. He told me that he would take it into consideration. During the termination meeting, Larry not only asked us to leave by the end of the year, he also coldly remarked that I would not even be considered for a teaching position, even though there was one available at the time. I questioned my skills as both a teacher and a youth care worker. Of the nearly twenty years I was a teacher, I started questioning my God given talents and abilities. Was it possible that I was no longer called to be a teacher? When I wasn't able to get a job after I was fired, I resorted to low brow jobs like selling substandard insurance and working on the internet. I didn't have the gift of manipulation to succeed as an insurance salesman and the internet job was a legal fiasco. The long and short of it was that I was hired as a teacher after Dark Hills told me that I wasn't a teacher of their choosing. I learned that God does not take away your gifts unless you squander them. The other cliché is that God does not close doors without opening a window. Stay faithful to Him and He will provide.

The final lesson learned is that organizations have no desire to change, especially if the directors are close minded. As a department head, I remember talking to one of my staff members who was having a particularly difficult time adjusting to Bright Meadows and following the procedures. It was apparent he was not happy and seemed to oppose anything I suggested. Although I was not necessarily encouraging him to leave, I asked him why he would want to work in a ministry that he obviously had disdain for. He told me that he felt called by God to be an agent of change for Bright Meadows. I informed him that even as a department head I couldn't make changes as easily as he desired. The staff member also did not realize that in order to be an agent of change, you have to gain the trust and respect of not only the leaders and directors, but also the staff you work with. The only way people can make real changes is to open their own business or organization.

As much as my wife and I went through at Dark Hills Academy, I don't believe that my wife and I made the wrong decision to accept the house parenting position. The only thing that we could have done differently was go through the interview process of the second child care facility that was interested in us at the same time we were interviewing at Dark Hills. Dark Hills actually hired us first, so the second interview at the other school seemed superfluous. We also would have had to provide our own housing at the other school, which would have been more stressful. If the job didn't work out there, we would have had two house mortgages to worry about. Besides, everything seemed ideal to accept the position offered to us.

To me, looking for a position at a residential youth care facility is like buying a cantaloupe. Most of them look appealing if you don't know how to look for a good one, but once you purchase it, there's no returning it. It could be the ideal fruit or it could be rotten on the inside, leaving you with no other option but to dispose of it. As Jesus pointed out in His Word, "By their fruits you may know them."

PROGRAMS UNDER PRESSURE

There is no question in my mind that there is a great demand for residential child care facilities like Bright Meadows Academy or Dark Hills Academy. All one has to do is look at the large number of talk shows and reality shows that focus on parents that are unable to control their children and teenagers. Guidance counseling and child psychology is always an option, but some students are too wily or unwilling to work with a psychologist. This would explain the very large number of these organizations all over the United States, from New England to California. Many of these facilities also carry the "Christian" label with denominations ranging from Baptist to Church of Christ. Even though there is a great need for youth care facilities, it would seem to make sense that residential youth care work is a marketable and secure career choice. Although there may be organizations that are considered successful, there are many others that are either struggling or very close to closing, if they haven't done so already.

Although youth care work is a ministry, the organization itself is a business as well. As with any business, one of the biggest issues concerns money. Most residential schools are non-profit, which means that their goal is not to make a profit. They are either privately funded by the students' care givers or are given money through grants or donations. In their infancy, most of these organizations are presented to church boards as good ideas and the board takes it upon themselves to help the visionary with the good idea to help fund the project. This is why so many of these facilities are affiliated with a particular church. Some organizations were started by celebrities or other people of notoriety. Since there are many glitches to work out, the first few years are usually the most difficult and poorly run. However, as directors and supervisors learn from their mistakes and as procedures are established, the subsequent years run smoother. Student enrollment also increases as positive word-of mouth spreads. If it is a poorly run organization and changes aren't made, the program will not last.

Youth care facilities not only have to come up with the money to pay for their organization initially, they have to keep coming up with the money to keep it going. It is mind boggling just how much money it costs to keep these institutions going. Bright Meadows, for example, cost parents a few thousand dollars a month to keep their business going. Needless to say the majority of the students who attended Bright Meadows belonged to the upper echelon of society, i.e. doctors, lawyers, and well-paid professionals. Although they accepted charity cases once in a while, that money had to come right out of the care giver's own pocket; these places are usually not covered by health insurance. Sadly, I have seen many parents, or at least heard of parents, taking out second mortgages on their houses, cashing in life insurance policies, or using up various family funds just so their rebellious child can go to that particular school. Other Christian organizations appeal to the benevolence of affluent churches to obtain the money they need. It's interesting to note how many of these child care facilities are located around the state of Texas. One theory is that these organizations get many of their donations from churches whose members are in the oil industry.

As shocking as the amount of money is, schools have to charge high tuitions or require generous donations in order to pay their staff the income they deserve. Most organizations may offer health care benefits or other incentives like annual salary increases to entice quality staff. Of all the expenses a school has, personnel is the highest percentage of their expenses. On rare occasions, particularly with overseas schools, a staff member may be required to raise their own funds to pay for their living expenses. In other words, the prospective worker presents their mission to various churches and the churches decide whether or not to financially support that person in the work that they do. The majority of the house parents in the United States are paid like regular employees and don't have to do this. I also heard stories of staff members who were unable to receive their pay because the organization lacked sufficient funds. It was interesting that in this story, the teachers and house parents went without their pay while the administration still received theirs.

Needless to say, the financial burden of any residential facility, Christian or otherwise, is omnipresent. Now more than ever, the monetary strain that these places are under is Herculean and getting worse every year. With the recession and rising cost of living, families just don't have the money to pay for these organizations anymore. Moreover, people's donations also dwindle because they are seen as a needless expense. During a financial crisis, charities are usually the first to be hit and are hit the hardest. Even government funding is no longer a sure thing. My wife worked for a residential mental health treatment facility before we became house parents. Although they were supported by government money, the government was very poor in providing the money they needed. As a result, many of these places are either drastically down-sizing or shutting their doors altogether. A representative of the Association of Christian Schools International (ACSI) made a comment about four years ago that he has seen an alarming number of Christian schools shut their doors because they were no longer able to afford the expenses. Still other places have no additional donations coming in and are using the last of their financial resources.

Money management for these kinds of residential schools is no easy task, but it is essential to keep the school afloat. So many of these directors do a fantastic job being the visionary for the program, but they make many poor decisions when it comes to finance. Some directors accept students from families who cannot pay, and thereby causing a strain on their budgets. Of course, the more students whose families cannot pay, the greater the strain is on the organization. Other places hire staff members whom they cannot pay. Even little expenses, like utilities and food, can create great financial stress if needlessly squandered. Some places hire a financial advisor or a person in charge of fund raising to help alleviate some of the monetary stress. It is ironic that these people are usually the most expensive people on the organization's payroll. For example, the fund raiser for Dark Hills made double the amount of money as my wife or I did working as house parents.

As much as I loved working as a teacher at Bright Meadows, I began seeing some very disturbing trends. The most obvious one was our enrollment. When I transferred up to the American campus, there were five student houses open, all of which were full. By 2003, however, they only had three student houses open. Even though they tried to run four houses in 2007, they just didn't have the student numbers to support four houses. Our summer program, which usually ran twelve to sixteen students, only had three students in 2008. By the time I left in 2009, there were only two houses open: one boy's house and one girl's house. The sister schools in Canada and the Caribbean were also suffering from low enrollment. The American and Canadian campuses eventually closed down, but the Caribbean program is still open, though the enrollment is dangerously low.

There is an old saying that desperate times call for desperate measures. For the last four years of my employment, Bright Meadows had a hiring freeze (no new staff were hired) and present staff members did not receive annual pay increases. Even if staff members resigned, they had no intention of hiring replacements, unless there was a need for new house staff. Consequently, this meant that the staff members that were still working there had more responsibilities to their long lists of duties. By the end of 2008, I counted at least ten staff members who were laid off in the month of December alone. It was at this time that my wife and I decided to look for work elsewhere; I knew it was only a matter of time before I would be laid off. After I left, staff were asked to take a 20% reduction in pay; some administrators willingly took a 25% reduction in pay. Even Dark Hills Academy had to lay off their only licensed teacher on account of not having the funds to keep him on the payroll. In these organizations, teachers and support staff like counselors and chauffeurs are usually the first ones to go. House parents, on the other hand, are usually the last ones to go, since they are the ones who have to stay on duty, regardless of the number of students. By this point, there is a genuine fear that the school is in great jeopardy.

During these times the school climate changes for the worst. Layoffs add an element of fear and uncertainty, making both staff and students tenser. It was interesting to see an increase in group misbehavior during this time. It was as though the students knew that there was a decrease in staff supervision and felt like they could get away with more. Less reputable places actually created reasons to fire staff so they would not have to pay unemployment. During a massive layoff, the human resources department accused a staff member of lying on her resume. What made this investigation suspicious was the fact that it was the timing of the investigation as well the fact that the staff member had been employed for well over a year. I also heard stories of workers being fired for either standing up for other staff members' rights or for making helpful suggestions.

In addition to financial pressures, youth care facilities also have to face pressures from government agencies and licensing processes. Any time there were whispers of a government inspection, the campus would go into a frenzy of cleaning and rearranging. What's interesting is that at Dark Hills, the students who received preferential treatment from the administrators made the most fuss to get the cottage clean. Any other day the same student would make a poor effort to clean. What made inspections especially stressful is that if an organization receives a poor inspection, they are labeled as an at-risk place. Once this label is in place by the state, it is seldom, if ever, removed.

If any kind of sexual abuse or legal allegations are made against the school, the government agencies will always view the school with suspicion.

Even though schools and residential facilities benefit greatly from accreditation and licensing, it can also add to the amount of stress. One of the things that families look for to place their child are credentials an organization might have. Of course the more reputable the credentials, the more arduous the accreditation process is. It took literally years to complete the accreditation process for ACSI for all three of our campuses. Once the process is complete, it is up to the school to act on the recommendations made based on the visit. Depending on the urgency of the recommendation, if a school does not make the required changes, they run the risk of losing their accreditation. Sadly, Bright Meadows lost theirs because they did not have the funds required to make the necessary changes. For a school to be licensed by the state, it must have licensed teachers, which many Christian schools cannot afford.

Accreditation and licensure may also require a residential facility to function in such a way that goes against their philosophies. For example, many licensing committees frown upon corporal punishment and may put stipulations on what kind of punishment an organization uses. If a student has to be restrained for behavioral outbursts, it must be done in accordance to policies laid out by the state. Failure to do so could result in intensive investigations, and even termination of the employee. It is therefore the organization's responsibility to train their staff members in how to handle disciplinary issues effectively and in accordance to state regulations. In order to prevent legal hassles, the Canadian program of Bright Meadows told the Canadian government that their summer program was actually a recreational camp. When they decided to be certified by a certain association, the association insisted on observing the Canadian program. Although that was not a problem in and of itself, the association was told that the Canadian program was a disciplinary school and not a recreational camp. All the association had to do was talk to the Canadian government for Bright Meadows to be asked to leave the country. To prevent this, Bright Meadows had to adapt a more permissive disciplinary philosophy.

Someone suggested to me recently that I ought to open up my own residential child care facility since I knew so much about how programs like this should run. Needless to say I gave an emphatic "no", even though I was flattered by the compliment. I believe that in this day and age, organizations like these face more financial and legal pressures than ever before. In short, the demand is there, but the money isn't. Not only that, but we live in a society that disapproves of austere discipline and that is bogged down by excessive amounts of bureaucracy and regulations. As long as an organization can prove that their clients are being disciplined and treated fairly, they should not have to be excessively harassed and micromanaged. Sadly, I don't see a very bright future for youth care facilities. In fact, unless dramatic changes happen to the economy and to government and youth care associations, youth care facilities face an uncertain future.

CONCLUSION

When I started at Bright Meadows Academy, I was clueless about residential child care facilities and did not realize there were different types of Christian schools. At the time, I simply wanted a teaching job with an opportunity to live in a different setting. I found out the hard way that residential facilities are nothing like a regular school I was anticipating. Unlike regular teachers, the work is much more intensive because the students are much higher maintenance. Another difference between working at a more traditional school and working at a residential facility is the main area of focus. Even though there is quite a bit of supervision required for any school or youth care facility, students who act out much more need more watchful eyes and stricter discipline. Consequently, staff members feel much more drained than regular teachers.

As I look back on my experience, I realize that youth care work is not a job, it is a ministry. An administrator once challenged us in a speech he gave that if all we wanted was a job then we were in the wrong area of work. He was right. Whether you are a teacher, a house parent, or any other kind of worker in a residential organization, your life is no longer your own. I honestly don't understand how workers who are not Christians are able to find the spiritual fortitude to do this kind of work in places that are not Christian. Workers have to have a clear focus on their mission and not be blindsided by the issues mentioned in this writing. The benefits and the income may not be as much as a secular organization, but if a worker has a clear vision and mission statement, the reward comes with knowing that you are making a difference in the lives of troubled souls.

Even with a clear mission statement and a desire to help others, the life of a youth care worker can be filled with stress, anxiety, and discouragement. This is why the turnover rate for these kinds of schools is much higher than a more traditional Christian school. For house parents, the turnover rate is even higher. No matter how efficiently run an organization is, the stress of working with at-risk teenagers is a stressful job. Unlike teachers, house parents are unable to fully get away from the job setting, since the majority of them live right on campus. There are the rare cases, however, that house staff stay on for longer than the obligatory two years. Most staff that stay longer usually transfer to other departments or positions. Organizations that require non-house staff to work in the house have a higher turnover rate than those that don't. Based on my personal experience, the turnover rate for house staff living overseas was about the same as that of staff members living in the United States. Teachers that teach overseas, of course, want to get back to the United States to settle into a job that is in their native country.

There are two basic things that will determine the effectiveness of the child care facility: their mission statement and their administration. If the organization has a philosophy or church denomination that does not match yours, it's not a good idea to accept a position. Otherwise your ministry will end in frustration and disappointment. It's also important that the administration does an effective job of taking care of discipline and supporting the staff members. An organization that does not show respect for the staff or effectively control its students is not worth working for.

All jobs, ministry and otherwise, have a certain amount of troubles and struggles associated with it. However, if the troubles and struggles outweigh the rewards and sense of accomplishment for an extended period of time, if might be an indicator that it is time to leave. Moreover, if the administration belittles, humiliates, and chides their staff frequently and rudely, this may also be an indication that it is time to move on. Joe, one of my supervisors at Dark Hills, seemed to be constantly reprimanded by Ron. Joe worked there for over seven years, but he was no more respected than the new staff like us who were only there for a year or so. I had a candid conversation with Joe, who told me that it was always a good idea to have a back-up plan. He told me that he was waiting for the right opportunity to leave Dark Hills and would as soon as that opportunity came along. In my opinion, people need to look for opportunities and not wait for them. This is why so many people are stuck in jobs and ministries that they loathe. As I stated earlier I do not believe God calls us to a life of dissatisfaction and misery; if He truly called us into a particular ministry, we should experience a sense of fulfillment, regardless of life's struggles.

As a Christian, it's important to keep your spiritual life strong. House parents can experience feelings of isolation and loneliness, even though they have their spouse and family to turn to. God should always be the center of your life and ministry; otherwise, frustration and misery is inevitable. Keeping close to the Lord can also help you make important decisions, like what type of ministry to go into, which organization to work for, and whether or not to stay or go from the particular facility you work at.

Nobody can make the decision for you as to work for a residential youth care facility or not. Ron once told me that Dark Hills Academy was not for everybody. Although he meant it in a condescending way, he was right. Working with troubled children is a very difficult line of work not intended for everybody. All of the times I spent working with young people can best be described by Charles Dickens in <u>A Tale of Two Cities</u>: "It was the best of times, it was the worst of times ..." I learned quite a bit from my experiences through both satisfaction and contentment as well as through pain and tears. So far as my future calling, I honestly don't feel like God is calling me into the same types of ministries like Bright Meadows Academy or Dark Hills Academy. However, things could change and God could call me back. If that ever happens, I hope to follow the rules, lessons, and suggestions I presented to you.